The Philosophy of Friendship

Mark Vernon

8/16/06
ww
35 -

First published 2005 by
PALGRAVE MACMILLAN
Houndmills, Basingstoke, Hampshire RG21 6XS and
175 Fifth Avenue, New York, N.Y. 10010
Companies and representatives throughout the world

PALGRAVE MACMILLAN is the global academic imprint of the Palgrave Macmillan division of St. Martin's Press, LLC and of Palgrave Macmillan Ltd. Macmillan® is a registered trademark in the United States, United Kingdom and other countries. Palgrave is a registered trademark in the European Union and other countries.

ISBN-13: 978–1–4039–4874–8   hardback
ISBN-10: 1–4039–4874–7   hardback

This book is printed on paper suitable for recycling and made from fully managed and sustained forest sources.

A catalogue record for this book is available from the British Library.

Library of Congress Cataloging-in-Publication Data
Vernon, Mark, 1966–
    The philosophy of friendship / Mark Vernon.
        p. cm.
    Includes bibliographical references and index.
    ISBN 1–4039–4874–7 (hardcover)
    1. Friendship. I. Title.
BJ1533.F8V47 2005
77'.62–dc21   2005046345

10   9   8   7   6   5   4   3   2   1
14   13   12   11   10   09   08   07   06   05

Printed and bound in Great Britain by
Antony Rowe Ltd, Chippenham and Eastbourne

In memory of
Susan Frances Vernon

Contents

Acknowledgements

This book is in part a product of friendships, amongst whom I think of Denise Inge, Craig Mackenzie, Jeremy Carrette, Guy Reid, Chris Biddle, Paul Fletcher, John Inge, Angie Hobbs and Richard Jenkins. I must thank other individuals who have read various chapters and drafts, notably Michael Savage, James Davidson and particularly Lisa Mackenzie. Great thanks also goes to those who signed me up and then steered the book through at Palgrave, especially Luciana O'Flaherty, Dan Bunyard and Lisa Dunn, and also to my copy-editor, Peter Andrews. Underpinning all is the love and friendship of Nick.

Acknowledgements

Introduction: the Ambiguity of Friendship

Their relationship consisted
In discussing if it existed.
                    Thom Gunn

For a long time I was single. I relied heavily on friends for company, support and affection. And most of the time I was happy about that. Implicitly, I agreed with Aristotle: who would choose to live without friends even if they had every other good thing, he said. Moreover, I regarded myself as exceptionally lucky with my friends and still do.

But for all that, I was often alone and sometimes lonely. The friendships I enjoyed only went so far.

The limits were most obvious when compared to the relationships I witnessed between lovers or within families. It seemed to me that notwithstanding the occasional exception, friendship simply cannot bear the demands and intimacies, great and small, that are the very stuff of these other relationships of love and blood.

This set me thinking because my experience seemed very different from the way friendship is portrayed at a cultural level. Here it is frequently heralded as nothing less than the defining relationship of our age. In TV soaps, the characters always have their friends to return to when their sexual adventures fail; lovers come and go, but friends remain. Or, according to agony aunts, friendship is the ingredient that makes partnerships work (a suggestion that would have surprised many of those same agony aunts' aunts who ironically might have suggested the ingredient of partnership to make relationships work). For sociologists, a common assumption is that friendship is now most people's relationship of choice, and people often see their friends in opposition to traditional relationships of obligation: as marriage and family flounders, to say nothing of lifestyles becoming more mobile, the belief (or hope) is that friendship will carry them through the serial monogamies and speedy pace of life. And for politicians, the idea of civic friendship is also gaining ground. Here the thought is that modern democracy can be revivified by a notion of citizenship that includes a concern for others' wellbeing. Such civic friendship would counterbalance the dominant economic and individualistic model of politics which is mostly about rules and rights, and therefore tends to marginalise the civic space.

All in all, friendship is conceived of positively, as the new social glue to paste over networked lives: because it is ideally structured to cope with the stresses and strains, great and small, that modern life throws up, it will stop them falling apart.

But will it? My experience told me that whilst friendship can be great, its affections and commitments are often ambiguous. When a lover calls they automatically get first priority and family commitments are, well, family commitments. So perhaps the soaps are romanticising friendship, the agony aunts are resorting to it too quickly, and the sociologists and politicians are being overly optimistic?

In fact, this question is also regularly debated in the same TV programmes, newspaper columns, learned journals and political speeches. It is not one that will be decided here. However, upon further reflection it seemed to me that another, perhaps even more fundamental, question is rarely being asked – and it is one with which philosophy should be able to help. What exactly is friendship? What is its nature, its rules, its promise? How can one differentiate between its many forms? How does it compare to and mix with the connections shared between lovers and within families? If at least a kind of friendship is elastic enough to survive the relational stresses and strains of our flexible ways of life, is that friendship also strong enough to bear the burden of the human need to belong, to be connected, to be loved?

These questions are trickier to answer than it might first seem because friendship is hugely diverse. Although it is relatively easy to come up with definitions that account for part of it, it is much harder to find one that does not exclude any of its facets. Aristotle, whose writing on friendship still sets the philosophical agenda to this day, found as much 2,500 years ago. Friendship, he proposed, is at the very least a relationship of goodwill between individuals who reciprocate that goodwill. A reasonable starter for ten. However, as soon as he tried to expand it, the definition seemed to unravel.

He looked around him and saw three broad groupings of relationships people called friendship. The first group are friends primarily because they are useful to each other – like the friendship between an employee and a boss, or a doctor and a patient, or a politician and an ally; they share goodwill because they get something out of the relationship. The second group are friends primarily because some pleasure is enjoyed by being together; it may be the football, the shopping, the gossip or sexual intimacy, but the friendship thrives insofar, and possibly only insofar, as the thing that gives the pleasure continues to exist between them. Aristotle noted that these first two groups are therefore like each other because if you take the utility or the pleasure away, then the chances are the friendship will fade.

This, though, is not true of the third group. These are people who love each other because of who they are in themselves. It may be their depth of character, their innate goodness, their intensity of passion or their simple *joie de vivre*, but once established on such a basis these friendships are ones that tend to last. Undoubtedly much will be given and much taken too but the friendship itself is independent of external factors and immensely more valuable than the friendships that fall into the first two groups.

That there are better or higher friendships – different people may call them soul friends, close or old friends, or best friends – as opposed to instrumental and casual friendships, or mere friendliness, is surely right. But to say that great friendship is defined solely by its goodwill seems to miss its essence. Goodwill exists in these best kinds of friendship, but, unlike the lesser types, best friendship – arguably the quintessential sort – is based on something far more profound.

Aristotle recognised as much, and whilst his discussion of friendship contains many important and illuminating insights – that we will make much of here – he knew, I think, that ultimately a definitional approach to friendship has its limits.

This philosophical ambiguity as to what friendship is reflects, then, the ambiguity that appears to be part and parcel of friendship in life. Try listing some of the friends you have – your partner, oldest friend, mates or girlfriends, one or two family members, work colleagues, neighbours, friends from online chat rooms, family friends, a boss perhaps, therapist, teacher, personal trainer – whoever you might at some time think of as a friend. A look at such a list puts your friends in front of you, as it were, and highlights the vast differences. For example, the friendship with your partner will in certain key respects be unlike that of your oldest friend, though you may be very close to both. Conversely, although friendship is for the most part a far less strong tie than say the connection to family, you may feel less close to members of your family in terms of friendship than others with whom you have no genetic or legal bond. Then again, lovers might make you blush and families can make you scream, but friendship – even soul friendship – is usually cool in comparison.

As you continue further down the list to the friends who are in many ways little more than acquaintances, associates or individuals for whom you have merely a sense of friendliness, it is obvious that friendship stretches from a love you could scarcely do without to an affection that you'd barely miss if it ended. Some people would say there is some minimal quality which means that it makes sense to call all of them friends (perhaps Aristotle's goodwill). Others would disagree: they are the sort who say they have a handful of friends and that others are people they only know. In other words, the ambiguity of friendship extends to the very possibility of prolific and profound friendship-making.

Personally, I think that Aristotle is on to something in his belief that the closest kind of friendship is only possible with one or two individuals, such is the investment of time and self that it takes. 'Host not many but host not none', was his formula. He would argue that less is more and it is easy to substitute the networking for the friendships it is supposed to yield. One of my arguments will be that life produces personal relationships of many types, but out of these connections good friendship may or may not grow. For example, certain associations or institutions like work or marriage can foster friendship but those same associations or institutions need not necessarily be characterised by friendship themselves; friendship emerges, as it were, from below up. It is a fluid concept.

Another dimension to the ambiguity of friendship is its apparent open-endedness. Unlike institutions of belonging such as marriage which is supported and shaped by social norms, or work where individuals have contractually defined roles, friendship has no predetermined instructions for assembly or project for growth. People have to create their friendships mostly out of who they are, their interests and needs, without any universally applicable framework. On the one hand, this is a potential weakness, because a friendship may 'go nowhere' or 'run out of steam'. On the other, it is a potential strength because there is also a freedom in this that is crucial to friendship's appeal: it is part of the reason for the diversity within the family of relationships called friendship.

In summary, then, it seems that it is not possible to say unequivocally what friendship is. Sometimes it is intense, sometimes it is thin. Sometimes it appears to embrace many, sometimes only a few.

This might seem to be a bit of a blow if the question is what is friendship. However, far from ambiguity automatically leading to philosophical impasse, an exploration of the very ambiguities of friendship is actually a very good way forward. After all, is not mistaking relationships for what they are not – that is being blind to their ambiguity – arguably the greatest cause of disappointment and failure? A married couple may assume they are friends in some deep sense when really they only have goodwill for each other because of the kids; without realising that, when they go, the friendship does too. An employee and a boss may think they are good friends after all the late nights, trips abroad and hours spent together: but when the day arrives for the appraisal or pay rise, and both turn out to be modest, the friendship stumbles and falls.

Alternatively, consider this thought experiment suggested by Nietzsche:

> Just think to yourself some time how different are the feelings, how divided the opinions, even among the closest acquaintances; how even the same opinions have quite a different place or intensity in the heads of your friends than in your own; how many hundreds of times there is occasion for misunderstanding or hostile flight. After all that, you will say to yourself: 'How unsure is the ground on which all our bonds and friendships rest; how near we are to cold downpours or ill weather; how lonely is every man!'

Honesty about any relationship is likely to improve it, even if the honest thing to do is not put too much hope in it!

The mistakes that people can make in friendship are also exemplified in some of the things people commonly say about it. For example, many would say that the test of good friendship is being able to pick up immediately where you left off even if you haven't seen the friend for some time. Aristotle, though, thought that good friendship depends on shared living and spending substantial, regular, quality time together. 'Cut off the talk, and many a time you cut off the friendship,' he said. The question is where does the balance lie?

Or again, are not the Life columns of newspapers and magazines increasingly scattered with tales of friendship's labour lost? A piece on 'Google grief' caught my eye, the twenty-first century phenomenon of learning of the death of an old friend on the web. The writer, Michele

Kirsch, complained that having had such a shock, she was not allowed to grieve for her dead friend because those with whom she lived now were implicitly asking, 'If he was so brilliant, why haven't you been in touch for 18 years?' Fair question, she is forced to admit; the friendship she had was nostalgic and only in her head.

And yet, if it is really quite easy to make mistakes by thinking the relationship is something other that what it is, the best kinds of friendship (however that is judged) are essential for a happy life: human beings need people they can call friends and not just people who are relatives, partners, acquaintances, colleagues or associates. In other words, the corollary of friendship's ambiguity is that it is packed with promise and strewn with perils. This, then, sets the agenda for this book. It is these perils and that promise which I hope to track down, the ambiguities and points of contention that I address. My aim is not to try to produce a comprehensive definition or theory of friendship. Rather, the value of asking about friendship lies in the asking, not necessarily in coming to any incontestable conclusions.

I am taking a lead here from Plato. According to him, at the end of a lengthy conversation on friendship with the Greek youths Lysis and Menexenus, no less a person than Socrates concluded that he had not been able to discover what friendship was. He feared looking ridiculous because paradoxically it also seemed that he, Lysis and Menexenus were friends. But he had good reason for not tying friendship down. Although everyone has friends of some sort and friendships appear to share similarities, and thus be definable, they are in life as varied as the people who form them. This is the irreducibility of friendship; people have an infinite variety of experiences of it. So another way of putting it is that this is a philosophy book of the sort which invites you to test its ideas against your experience. (In fact, with a subject like friendship it is almost impossible to do otherwise.) It is a search through philosophy for the things that may thwart friendship and for the conditions within which it may best thrive.

Philosophy is frequently overlooked as a resource for thinking through friendship in this way. This has much to do with the fact that only a relatively small number of philosophers have written on the subject at any length. What is more, those that have, although generally agreeing that friendship is essential for a happy life, also say that it provides no automatic satisfaction of human desires for deeper relationships or society's need for connection. Friendship is 'a problem worthy of a solution', as Nietzsche gnomically put it. Or as Aristotle wrote: 'The desire for friendship comes quickly. Friendship does not.'

The implication is that the best kinds of friendships are only possible between people who properly value it and who understand how many things from the personal to the political can compromise, undermine and destroy it. There is an art to friendship. The hope is that philosophy can teach something about it.

Each chapter looks, therefore, at key ambiguities that may exist in any friendship, and almost certainly in certain types, to test for the perils and identify the promise.

The first begins with the world of work because work friends frequently exhibit some of friendship's chief ambiguities. For example, on the one hand, the workplace is a good place to find and make friends. But, on the other, it is also one where supposed friends can show remarkable indifference (as in the speed with which the friendship is forgotten when someone leaves the office). The workplace also has an insidious capacity to undermine friendship. The fly in the ointment is the culture of utility that pervades it. People are there to do things, they are paid for doing them, and they are often encouraged to compete against each other in so doing.

Now, although all friends use each other from time to time, this means that friends at work are at risk of coming to feel that they are merely being used. Therein lies the ambiguity of friendship at work. Moreover, the workplace is not an isolated environment in the Western world. It informs a culture that tends to colour society as a whole; productivity often counts for more than perspicacity, the professional touch more than the personal touch, being praised more than being praiseworthy, wherever you are. All this is detrimental to friendship and so this chapter also provides us with a first look at friendship in a social context.

The second chapter considers another source of ambiguity in friendship, namely, sex. The downside is that sex can clearly imperil friendships by its possessiveness or its inappropriateness. The upside is that a friendship which includes a sexual element is the best sort of relationship that many people hope to have. I will argue that the key is to recognise that whilst a sexual relationship will start with physical passion, a passion of a non-sexual sort needs to kick in too if a good friendship is to develop. This is actually a natural if at times delicate step to take because the two kinds of passion are connected: a mature couple will realise that their deeper desires cannot be satisfied only in each other and that their relationship should nurture a search for fulfilment elsewhere too, in wider aspirations and achievements shared together.

This chapter is also a good place to consider a related sort of friendship, passionate friendships that have never had a sexual element (and where to have gone down the sexual route would have destroyed it). The erotic element is here sublimated in the passion that these friends share; we say these friends have a passion for life.

Work and sex are two sources of ambiguity and the third chapter turns to another, exhibited in the way in which friends dissimulate. I am talking here about 'loving deceptions' such as when an individual says they like their friend's new boy- or girlfriend when they do not, or when someone else says that their friend's cooking or clothing or opinion is good or right when they really think it is wrong or bad. Once you start thinking about it, it becomes apparent that these false colourings, evasions and occasionally out-and-out lies pervade friendship. Even close friends will routinely dissimulate because they judge that the time is not right to speak out, that current sensitivities are too great for the honest truth, or more humbly that, even though they are close, equivocation is best because one should not presume to judge another's heart. The particularly odd thing about friendship is that this dissimulation, this feigning friendship, is often necessary for the friendship's sake. The question is what does this say about it? It turns out that the answer again has a plus, for it reveals another aspect of what is possible in the best kinds of friendship. This, in turn, is nothing less than a reflection on what it is to be human itself.

A different kind of ambiguity is explored in the fourth chapter, namely, the ambivalence with which ethics and moral philosophy tends to view friendship. It is marginalised for a number of reasons: ethic systems like utilitarianism or consequentialism do not know how to treat friendship because it seems to have ill-defined laws of its own; alternatively, the West's Christian inheritance has coloured certain secular institutions with a distrust of friendship because it is thought irredeemably selfish and particular. The question is whether this can be addressed philosophically and, then, redressed in practice.

This ambiguity also sets up a change of emphasis for the second half of the book, from the mostly personal to the mostly social. First, I ask why it is that although few philosophers have chosen to tackle the subject at any length, at certain times in the past friendship was a major concern (in ancient Athens, it was virtually on the core syllabus): what was it about friendship that led philosophers and theologians in the ancient and medieval worlds in particular to treat it seriously, when in modernity it is not? The suggestion is that in these periods of history, friendship enjoyed a social standing that it does not today. Ancient Greek political life seems to have incorporated quasi-institutions of friendship. The medieval world did so too, overlaying the fundamental social unit of the household. Such civic friendship stands in marked contrast to our own situation, in which friendship is thought of as an almost wholly private relationship. The philosophical question this chapter poses is what ideological changes to the detriment of civic friendship took place at the birth of modernity, and what has been lost as a result?

However, this is not to say that friendship carries no social or political weight today. Inasmuch as it does, though, it is of a very different sort. This is the politics of friendship that I look at in Chapter 6, in particular in the philosophies that are found in feminism and the women's movement, and more recently in gay and so-called queer thought. Essentially, the difference is that friendship is now viewed as subversive of social norms rather than constitutive of them as it was before. Think of the anxiety provoked by the idea of gay marriage: I will argue that this has little to do with sexual acts and much more to do with forms of friendship that challenge tight notions of family.

This chapter also raises the question of possible differences between the friendships of men and those of women. The evidence on this is mixed and hard to read. On the one hand, there are sociologists who have argued that intimacy has been transformed in the modern world: in the same way that distinct gender roles are eroding at a social level, so differences between male and female friendship are softening too. On the other hand, there are others who argue that the evidence shows that gendered patterns of friendship still form in childhood and continue into adult life: from this view follow conclusions such as that women's friendships are more to do with self-disclosure and empathy, whereas men's friendships are more about the sociability of enjoying or doing things together. This is a fascinating question and is one that we will come to from a philosophical perspective particularly in this chapter. (In other chapters, my assumption is that the ambiguities of friendship are likely to be experienced both by men and women, and that whilst it might be that gender plays a role, it is not determinative.)

If the modern politics of friendship wants things to be different at a social level, whether implicitly or explicitly, then the final chapter returns to the question of what friendship ultimately aims at on a personal level. I call this the spirituality of friendship, not least because the most profound kind of friendship that people hope for is often referred to as soul friendship. Having said that, this is, I think, a much misused and sentimentalised concept. The philosophical tradition portrays it as an exceptional and difficult love. It necessitates nothing less than being able to overcome the ambiguities of amity – though, if that is never wholly possible, it also suggests how one might live with regards to the very best that can be hoped for in friendship (which is much, if somewhat paradoxical).

So it turns out that philosophy is indeed illuminative of friendship. In the Conclusion I suggest why: at best, philosophy and friendship coincide – they are both founded upon the love that seeks to know.

The Appendix is for those who are interested in the philosophy of friendship in a more academic sense and addresses an issue that has been toyed with throughout the book – that of the rivalry, as I see it, between the account of friendship given by Aristotle and the portrayal of friendship as found in Plato. I want to suggest that in certain respects, and much against received wisdom, the latter is better. (For those interested in what particular philosophers have said on friendship, each chapter majors on the thought of one or a select few: Chapter 1 on Aristotle and Adam Smith; Chapter 2 on Plato and Aristotle; Chapter 3 on Nietzsche; Chapter 4 on Augustine, Kant and Thomas Aquinas; Chapter 5 on the ancient Greeks and Romans; Chapter 6 on feminism and Foucault; Chapter 7 on Montaigne, Emerson and Plato again).

And now, to work.

1
Friends at Work

In the desert no man meets a friend.
Eastern proverb

Many people say that they cannot watch *The Office*, the BBC's tragi-comic TV docudrama of life at work, because for all its laughs and for all its humanity, it makes them squirm. It is too close to life. It holds a mirror up to the endless hours people spend in strip-lit rooms and finds the experience wanting.

The friendship between the characters is never far from the surface of the plot. Or rather the edgy, forced relationships that often have to pass for friendship at work. As Tim, the sales rep, comments in one episode: you spend so much time with these people, more time than with your family, and yet you don't know them; all you might have in common with them is that you tread on the same carpet for eight hours a day.

Experience has made Tim sceptical. He has long nursed a love for Dawn, the receptionist. Everyone in the office knows about it and the agony it has caused him. And yet no-one is really able to care for him. Gareth, the team leader, wants to make light of it but, like everything else he does, he botches it and ends up just poking fun at Tim. The new woman, who sits opposite Tim, empathises but trivialises his love: wherever she works she is always fancied by blokes, she tells him with a smirk. Keith, in accounts, simply rides roughshod over his feelings by offering his, frankly, disgusting advice on how to win women. All in all, the people in the office cannot share Tim's burden, as true friends might, though they know all about it.

We might call this 'pseudo-intimacy', the state in which work colleagues can know so much about each other but can care so little.

11

However, pseudo-intimacy is not the fundamental problem with which relationships at work must contend. It is, I think, the product of a deeper ambiguity, one which *The Office* also portrays well. Here's another incident (taken from *The Office – Christmas Special* of 2003).

It features David Brent, the sacked regional manager and berk portrayed by Ricky Gervais. Since being sacked, he has taken to coming back to the office with his dog, to catch up with his former employees whom he calls friends. They 'listen in' as he holds court. Then Neil, the MD, comes in and bans David from the office for persistently wasting everyone's time. In protest, David appeals to his supposed office friends. To show Neil up for the inhumanity of banning a man who only wanted to visit his friends, he asks them, 'Who fancies a drink after work?' His request is met with silence. David pleads: he is free tomorrow. Silence. He is free Thursday. Silence. Finally, Tim, out of begrudging goodness, volunteers to go for the drink. David grimaces at Neil – the awkward expression of the Pyrrhic victor. He not only has no friends in the office but barely any allies.

It is a painful moment but the interesting question for us is why everyone stopped acting as friends the minute David asked them out for a drink? Were they not friendly before? The answer, I think, lies in the fact that prior to the invitation David gave them something they wanted – a distraction from the working day. He broke the tedium of the office. But to go for a drink with him after work would be a lot of hassle, with minimal pleasure, and no such return. Hence the ensuing silence. In other words, take his usefulness away and the friendliness towards him ceases too. Put more generally and we have the fundamental source of the ambiguity of most friendships at work. They are determined by their utility.

On being useful

People's utility at work extends way beyond just being a welcome distraction or even performing a role or a function. It goes to the heart of the work environment, underpinning why people are at work to start with. They are there to do something, for a client, for a team, for a boss. Moreover, work is not work without one key utility for the employee, namely, the pay cheque.

That utility is the fundamental operating principle in work relationships can be shown in a variety of ways (I am thinking for the moment of the majority of the relationships someone has at work: some people may just find that they like each other and as far as that is concerned basically ignore the fact that they are at work!). For example, when people are friendly with the boss, on top of being civil or polite, is it not at least in part because they depend on them for pay, for perks and for a peaceful life – that is, the utility the boss performs for them? Alternatively, why is it hard to resist disliking a colleague who doesn't pull their weight or someone else who makes work for others, even if they are otherwise perfectly nice people? Is it not because at work their likeability is determined by their ability to fulfil their role or function; fail there and friendliness will not follow. Or, why do people like the postman, the tealady or the receptionist? Is it not because they provide the service of being good for gossip and easing the day away? (Incidentally, research shows that gossip at work is good for your health, so office gossips really are doing something useful.) And what of perhaps the deepest conundrum of all. Why is it that you can have known a colleague for years, enjoyed their company day after day, worked with them, even helped them when personal matters spilt into the workplace, and yet, when they left, it was, overnight, almost as if you had never known them? The reason is that the relationship was at heart one of utility based mostly on what was done together. Take that away, which is what happens when people leave, and, like a flower cut, any friendship withers. It is not that they were not liked or had nothing in common with you. It is that the thing held in common, work, is gone; and without doing that together the relationship ceases to have reason or purpose.

The ambiguity of most work friends is also illustrated by what happens to colleagues if they happen to meet outside work. Many will have an inkling of just how unnerving, and amusing, this can be. Clearly few want to be spotted secretly scanning the job section in the newsagents or to be caught buying luxury moist toilet tissue in the supermarket. But what of this? You're in *Beds* at Ikea and through a stack of filing cabinets in *Home Office* see the person who sits across from you at work, in *Kitchens*. You spend eight hours a day in the same room and have only friendly feelings towards them. So why might you now put your head down, fake a thorough assessment of the quality of the mattresses, and give them time to move on? Alternatively, at the cinema, heading for the seats, your eyes meet those of someone you've worked with on many projects. You approach, all smiles, and then note: they are of the opposite sex. You have a flush of anxiety. Do you merely shake hands or exchange a kiss?

The reason for these embarrassments is that stripping work relationships of their utility takes away their *raison d'être*. So outside work, people find it hard to know how to relate to one another, apart from reverting to talk about work. They become awkward because the framework within which they conduct the relationship is gone. (Or they simply don't want to see their colleagues because no matter how nice they might be, they only remind them of work.) Even if your relationships at work include a drink at the end of the day or can cope with a casual encounter at the weekend, there will be limits to what they can sustain. This is why team-building away days are so dreaded. The fear is that they overstep the mark by putting people together as if they were friends. They are often only saved by the identification of a common enemy, the facilitator or boss, whom as the recipient of mutual animosity creates the illusion of friendship in the group.

In fact, work is not the only place where these utility-type friendships predominate. Any friendship that is based primarily upon the fact of doing something together shares similarities with it. For example, political friends mostly have to do with politics – the art of doing the possible, we might say, with the emphasis on the utility-oriented doing. This is not to say that some politicians do not become very good friends; but for most the friendship lasts only so long as the political alliance or advantage does too. Alternatively, friendships based upon a common activity are the same, the utility being the benefit of doing whatever it is together. Friendships from those that form between charity workers to those that develop on reality TV shows are examples: take away the charitable work or the show and, for most, the friendship will fall away, if with a warm remembrance of what was shared or achieved in the past. Or again, friendships formed online in virtual communities of interest are like this too. The thing that drives the friendliness of the chat room is the mutual usefulness or common enthusiasm that the internet is so good at propagating. Few of those friendships, though, would transcribe into the real world where what is shared online does not dominate.

On not being used

Aristotle identified the principal characteristic of work friendships as he stalked the marketplaces of ancient Greece and Macedonia. He is hard to beat in his examination of the nature of these friendships, characteristic of 'business types', as he put it.

Those who are friendly with each other because they are useful to each other do not like each other for the person each one is in themselves. They like each other only insofar as it does them some good. They are friendly because it is beneficial to be so.

He identifies the heart of the matter. People are friendly with colleagues primarily because they are useful to them and not because they know anything much of the person as they are in themselves. Whence the weakness of the friendship and the reason it is a lesser type. The affection only goes as far as the benefit of being friendly itself and if they cease to perform some function or utility for you, because they are useless you might say, then the friendliness peters out: you have no other connection with them to draw on and sustain the friendship.

Think of the word 'friend' itself, and its conjugates – friends, friendly, friendliness, friendship. For example, I do a lot of freelance work and, consequently, work with a number of different people. I am more or less friendly with them all and imagine that my friendliness is one of the reasons they ask me to work for them again. When working together, we will enjoy friendly conversations, gossip or otherwise; many of them might say of me, 'He is a friend of the company'. Others might ask me, from time to time, to do them a favour, which I do, partly to generate goodwill that I hope might have some return in the future, and partly out of friendship. One or two individuals I work with might even call me 'friend' on occasion – perhaps at a Christmas party. But if I heard them describing me as *a friend*, say, to someone who was truly a friend of theirs, I would think that was overstepping the mark. I do not really know them, I would say: I am friends but not a friend. My friendliness might share attributes of a deeper friendship – such as trusting and liking one another to an extent. But it is nothing compared with friendship founded on the intimacy of knowing and loving someone well.

Now, when analysed in this way, it may seem that work relationships have more in common with the sycophancy of pleasing superiors or acts of self-interest than friendship. Perhaps the wise person should be sceptical of friendship at work or write it off altogether. To do so, though, would be to come down too quickly on work relationships because though they will all contain an element of utility that does not necessarily imply that they are all merely exploitative.

What is needed is a distinction between what we might call 'hard exploitation' and 'soft mutual benefit' in relationships. Unmoderated exploitation is never going to provide fertile grounds for friendship. But soft mutual benefit is not only bearable in work relationships but also actually common to all friendships. Indeed, even best friends are, in part, a good thing to have because of what they can do for you, for the function they can perform – from trivialities like feeding the cat, to being there to pick up the pieces when life falls apart. Some would say that the defining mark of a good friend is that they are always there for you and thus have a kind of unconditional utility. 'I'll be there, yes I will. You've got a friend', are James Taylor's words. The difference between that and relationships at work is that these latter people are friendly *mostly* because you are there for them. You are first liked not for who you are but for what you give.

At the same time, this means that the possibility of genuine friendship at work is not automatically excluded. A common project is an excellent way of bringing people together which must, on occasion, result in good friendship: people do come genuinely to like each other! Moreover, work may be one of the best sources of friends – as well as one of the most desirable places to have one. The point is that these relationships are always, at least at first, influenced by the utility factor. The trick is to ensure they are not determined by it.

This, though, is harder to do than might first meet the eye because the work environment throws up all sorts of hurdles to relationships based primarily on liking someone for who they are, not what they give. To see the extent of the problem we need to break the matter down into two constitutive elements. The first operates at a personal level: how to negotiate the debilitating impact of utility on friendship. The second operates at a broader, social level: why does the modern workplace cultivate such a powerful culture of utility and to what extent can friendship overcome it? Consider the personal dimension first.

On winning friends, not merely influencing people

Many of Aristotle's thoughts on friendship are focused on this problem. In Chapters VIII and IX of his *Nicomachean Ethics*, his most sustained piece of writing on the subject, he makes a number of suggestions as to tackling the ambiguities that utility puts on friends, at work and elsewhere. They stem partly from his analysis of such friendships and also from the tone he adopts when discussing them. This is important, I think: he has an attitude of unsentimental honesty. The point seems to be that it is vital to recognise work relationships for what they are. Right discernment will show the extent to which any friendship that they exhibit depends on what the individuals do together and the extent to which the friendship can be deepened into knowing, liking and maybe even loving the individual for who they are themselves.

However, there are a number of quite subtle factors that can impede such progress. Therein lies the real challenge. First, Aristotle notes that friendships of utility are both easy to form and can then easily be confused with deeper friendship. They are easy to form for the reason that what brings the friends together does not come from themselves, which takes time to share, but from the work, which is shared immediately (this might be the camaraderie of doing things together or, conversely, the solidarity found in both not wanting to be there). Now, such feelings undoubtedly humanise the workplace: the gossip over the photocopier or the emailed joke about the boss are vital. But this in itself is no indicator of the possibility for deeper friendship. For example, a mutually shared indiscretion may be taken as a sign of friendship. But there need be nothing necessarily very intimate about it when, again, it is founded on the shallow grounds of what the individuals do in common, not on the person they are in themselves. In fact, indiscretion can create an illusion of intimacy; such 'friends' may really be sounding boards not real confidants. Thus it can be mistaken for a deeper friendship.

Second, Aristotle sees that friendships characterised by utility are transient too: the things that bring the individuals together often change – be it the project, the gossip, or the job itself – and in quite arbitrary ways. Once that happens any friendship dissolves as well, for it existed only in relation to that which brought it about. Such transience, may mean that the relationship is over before there was even a chance for anything of any depth to take root.

Third, work friendships can be shaky because the individuals concerned do not always get the same thing out of the relationship. The office joker will demand an audience and think them friends but the supposed friend on the receiving end of these demands can easily just feel used. What is more, so-called friendships formed on this basis are not even necessarily with or between pleasant people. The friendships depicted in the movie *Trainspotting* are an extreme version of this, as the loser, the liar, the psycho and the junkie use and abuse each other. The workplace equivalents of the loser, the liar and the psycho are the careerist, the sycophant and the person who will walk over anyone in their way: they will be your friends, for as long as it suits them.

This leads us to another set of issues, around what happens when friendships at work go wrong. The problem here is that because they are conditional on bringing some benefit, they are also prone to accusation when that benefit is not, or is perceived to have not been, delivered. In the workplace, this can be dangerous. Not only has a possible friend been lost but also a possible enemy has been made. Once the damage is done and bad feeling has set in, one party may well have it in their power to spoil the other person's career prospects, for example. Backstabbing and insidious rumour can cause tremendous trouble. It is for this reason that sociologists of the workplace report that colleagues often pretend to remain friends with others even when they secretly despise them; they'd rather do that than risk animosity. Similarly, self-help books often advise avoiding friendships at work and letting no-one become more than an amicable acquaintance.

Even if people are not so objectionable, the omnipresence of utility can be confusing. It makes for another illusion of friendship that, again, is ambiguous. For example, a friendly character or admirable temperament might look like an attitude of friendship but is still actually subservient to the business of getting on at work. Or someone may show goodwill towards you that is nothing of the sort. This last possibility is known as the 'Hawthorne Effect', after an experiment done in Western Electric's Hawthorne factory in 1927. Investigators turned the lights up in the factory and worker productivity went up. They then turned the lights down in the factory and strangely productivity went up a little more. The conclusion they reached was that just an impression of care, of goodwill, makes workers more productive. In the same way, a letter of thanks from your boss will please you even if you know he doesn't particularly care for you.

Finally, discerning the friendliness of utility from true friendship is difficult because at work many people want to maintain a degree of privacy and are guarded about what they reveal of themselves. (For the same reason it is often deemed inappropriate to enquire into people's personal lives – unless, of course, someone has to because it affects their utility, as in the case of ill health.) The result is that on one level colleagues assume that they know a great deal about each other, as a by-product of spending all that time together, but on another level they actually understand little – the issue of pseudo-intimacy. Similarly, professionalism compromises the extent to which people can get to know each other too. Consider the way people dress: it is usually indicative of their sense of their worth to the company, not who they are in themselves. The experiments with 'dress-down Fridays' prove the point: many would rather wear their usual work clothes because it causes too much anxiety to think how they want to present themselves otherwise. The fear is of revealing too much; it mitigates against friendship.

So, looking at these problems as a whole, we can see that although an attitude of unsentimental honesty might seem a steely attitude for the fostering of friendship, it has the great advantage of enabling one to discern the amicable wheat from the utilitarian chaff and the relationships from which friendship can grow. If friendship is about knowing someone truly and being known by them, it is also about knowing which relationships are likely to foster good friendships; the relationships that contain the seeds of deeper friendship, as opposed to shallow, utilitarian friendliness. It all depends on the attitude people have to their utility and what they expect of others. But perhaps when genuine good feeling rises above mere benefit, an admiration for character over professional achievement, a virtuous spiral of regard can blossom into friendship.

The ultimate test: befriending bosses

Consider now a subset of the personal dimension of the work relationships that one must contend with, namely, that of friendliness with the boss. This is inevitably tricky. It may be that you like your boss, they like you, they like the work you do for them, and you the rewards you receive in return. But even such happy circumstance is rarely stable. At the heart of the relationship lies an imbalance – in terms of power, money and status – from which problems for friendship readily arise. In short, is it possible to be friends with the boss?

There are a number of factors here that we have touched on already. But specifically in relation to this issue, they can be broken down into three parts. First, how are the overtures of friendship that a boss may make to a subordinate to be understood, and the reverse – the friendliness of a subordinate towards the boss? Second, what of the complications that arise if and when work is, at least in part, rewarding for its own sake? And, last but not least, what of the business of working for friends?

To unpack this set of problems it is worth doing a little reverse engineering and thinking, first, about the structure of the relationship between employees and bosses. Aristotle is illuminating once more. He divides the relationship into two parts. One is a contractual part, namely, the terms on which someone is employed that has to do with tasks, time and money. The other is a goodwill part, that is, the human bit of the working relationship. The contractual part is, by definition, impersonal. Goodwill is where the potential for friendship lies. Unhappiness stems from the confusion of the two.

Thus, returning to our first issue of friendliness from bosses, the most common difficulties stem from the confusion that arises as to the nature of the demands that a boss may make. Are they made on the basis of the contractual part of the relationship or the goodwill part? It is often not easy to tell the difference. For example, if a paycheque is late or it is necessary to work after hours, does the boss call on goodwill or contractual leeway to cope with the immediate crisis? The answer is probably a bit of both.

The matter is compounded further because people are inconsistent when it comes to what they will put up with: typically, they say that they would be happy to act virtuously in theory and then usually choose what is most beneficial for themselves in practice. In relation to work, it might be an excellent thing to do the extra labour without expectation of reward or benefit. But when it comes to it, such virtuousness rapidly goes out of the window (another product of utility: one is primarily there not to practise goodwill but to collect the paycheque). Hence a boss might think an extra hour or two after work a small thing whereas an employee could well regard it as a big deal.

For all that, Aristotle identifies a general rule. When asking employees to go the extra mile, the boss should operate on the side of caution if they want to keep them sweet: financial compensation and clear thanks for what has been given forms the basis of best practice. Moreover, the payment and thanks must be offered voluntarily: that keeps the relationship free of the complications of delayed or unrequited returns. And it must be offered generously, for people vary in their assessment of what they think their efforts are worth: the boss who over-remunerates at the time will reap goodwill in time.

So much for the responsibility of bosses. What of the other situation, when employees ask for something, perhaps time off, and thereby call on the boss's goodwill? Different forces come into play. The fundamental issue is that because the boss is generally in a position to help, the situation is actually loaded against them morally speaking – a friend in need and all that. What is more, the boss may fear loosing what friendship they enjoy with their staff if they do not respond positively (and staff may well ask what worth there is in having a friend who is powerful if it does not deliver benefits, at least from time to time). What keeps the issue within the bounds of friendship are the principles of voluntarism and generosity again: a second rule comes to look very much like the first. When someone calls on the boss's goodwill and asks for a favour, the boss should act reasonably and give freely, and the employee should be reasonable and show gratitude freely. True friendship, as Aristotle puts it, does not place the scales centre stage.

What now of work that people enjoy and find rewarding? The complication here is that a job might be thought to be its own reward in large part. This leads to the assumption that friendship can flow more freely between managers and subordinates because financial utility is not such a big issue. Not so, says Aristotle. He tells the story of a lyre player at a party who was promised payment and more, the better he played. When dawn came, he asked for what he thought were his dues. However, his employer regarded himself as something of a connoisseur. After hearing such beautiful music he could not comprehend the demand for mere cash: 'Surely, the beauty of the playing is payment enough', he reasoned. 'Your playing is its own reward.' Unsurprisingly the lyre player did not see it that way, and departed bitter and disappointed.

The moral of the story is not that the lyre player did not enjoy making music: he may have taken more pleasure from it than anyone. Rather, it is that whilst the party-giver sought music, the lyre player sought a living, and though the former received what he wanted in good measure, the lyre player did not. Work may include its own rewards but for the employee working for someone else it is still a means to an end.

The final scenario to consider is that in which people work for a friend. Once more, the ambiguity of the roles played by individuals in this situation makes it tricky at the best of times. In particular, the money that will necessarily change hands has an inexorable ability to draw all value to itself, sapping the goodwill of even the strongest friendships. The situation is hardly different if the friend in question is not the wage payer, but rather, say, a line manager; being subordinate is quite enough to cause trouble.

Typically, the rot sets in unawares. For example, I once worked for a friend, an arrangement that started off very well. I was deeply grateful to them for the break it gave me; they were glad to offer me a generous share in the rewards of the business, and a good work/life balance. When asked about how it was going by other friends, I told them that we were the exception to the rule: money and friendship can mix!

But that was when the going was good. When the business was hit by a particularly deep cash-flow crisis, I fell into the unhappy confusion between contract and goodwill that Aristotle identifies. It was clear what friendship demanded of me: work for a while without pay. But cash-strapped, I was not able to do so. As it happened, this spared me the harder question of whether I was willing to work unsalaried, but, that aside, I could not deliver for goodwill's sake and I quit. My action inevitably called the friendship into question and things were never the same again. The moral of that story is work for your friend at your own peril.

In general, then, the advice at the personal level is that friendship flourishes best when it is not compromised by the utility of the work-place. If friendships do begin there, one should either not expect too much or quickly establish ways of deepening the friendship that have nothing to do with work whatsoever (this will also show the relation-ship up for what it is: if it is merely a work relationship then the attempt to form a deeper friendship will flounder; if it is truly a friend-ship, then it will flourish). The philosophical principle is that friend-ships which depend upon doing something together also depend upon the mutual benefit that comes from that. If the benefit is cut for some reason then the relationship will be too. Such is the fragility of utility-based friendship.

The social dimension: commercial culture and the challenge to friendship

If the workplace presents barriers to friendship that are difficult to negoti-ate at a personal level, then the broader culture of work and the econ-omic milieu in general present a challenge to friendship-making too. This is the second dimension of the impact that utility can have on friend-ship, namely, that the underlying ideals of a commercially-minded society – in which utility, competition, profit and exchange are highly valued – set a socio-economic climate that people's friendships must contend with too. To develop this aspect, we can turn to another thinker, one of the founding fathers of the modern workplace, Adam Smith.

Smith was actually an optimist about the impact that commerce would have on the opportunities for friendship. He believed commer-cial life to be democratic and egalitarian, especially when compared to the feudal society of deference and inequality that it pushed aside. Because the industrial economy is a great leveller, people therefore find themselves on a level too which means, he reasoned, that they have better opportunities for friendship.

> Among well-disposed people, the necessity or conveniency of mutual accommodation, very frequently produces a friendship not unlike that which takes place among those who are born to live in the same family. Colleagues in office, partners in trade, call one

another brothers; and frequently feel towards one another as if they really were so. Their good agreement is an advantage to all; and, if they are tolerably reasonable people, they are naturally disposed to agree. We expect that they should do so; and their disagreement is a sort of small scandal.

Although to the contemporary ear this sounds a bit like the conviviality of a Pall Mall club, Smith is, in fact, that rare thing amongst modern philosophers as a thinker who takes friendship seriously. He resorts to it particularly in his book *The Theory of Moral Sentiments.*

Here, he centres on the concept of sympathy, a notion of compassion, empathy and consideration that underlines the importance of love and friendship in his thought. Having said that, he uses it ambivalently. Sometimes he appears to take sympathy as meaning the full affectionate feeling that is naturally associated with friendship. At other times sympathy implies merely fellow feeling, as if it were little more than an opinion held in common. This ambivalence is significant, I think. It is as if love and friendship struggle against other less accommodating factors within commercial society, for all that Smith wishes it were otherwise. In other words, we are back again with the ambiguities of utility that exist in the workplace.

However, Smith was aware of this and he tried to come up with a theory which showed how people could be friendly not just because they found themselves on the level and involved in a common enterprise, but more powerfully because commercialism positively nurtures a culture of friendship too. First, he took an idea from Aristotle. Aristotle thought that happiness was the goal of life. It could be achieved by individuals of increasing moral perfection – people who were increasingly courageous, open-handed, witty and characterful. What is more, he thought that by virtue of having these characteristics, friendship should come their way too.

Smith took this link between a goal of life, individual characteristics and resulting friendship, and adapted it to the world he saw around him. First, he replaced the goal of happiness with social cooperation. If that seems a mediocre thing to aspire to then that is not to say that the virtues of social cooperation are themselves mundane: if anything quite the opposite, since social cooperation requires individuals to act justly, beneficently and prudently. Finally, when individuals do act in this way, he argued, they should attract friends.

The trouble, though, is that although the virtues of social cooperation may be admirable, it is not entirely clear that individuals will readily aspire to them (unlike happiness, which makes its own case as a goal in life). So Smith developed another idea that is not Aristotelian but which would, he hoped, motivate people nonetheless. It is called the 'impartial spectator'.

An impartial spectator is a fictional presence that sees everything an individual does, not to pass judgement, but in order that the individual, believing that they are being watched, will act in the best way they can. If the idea of such an observer seems somewhat fanciful, its very shadowiness is part of Smith's idea too. The point is that the impartial spectator will not satisfy the individual by merely praising them when they behave well; it is not an internalised father-figure. Rather, it operates more like a mirror to encourage the individual to see themselves as they truly are.

The aim is to cultivate the individual's desire not for praise, a questionable if understandable goal, but to cultivate the individual's desire to be praiseworthy, a higher aim that nurtures the development of the individual's character and actions. As Smith puts it: 'Man naturally desires, not only to be loved, but to be lovely.' This, then, is what will inspire individuals to act according to the values of social cooperation: they will seek to be praiseworthy, not merely praised. And in turn, because that praiseworthiness makes them lovely, they will find friends.

What is more, these people of good character should expect many good friends:

> Such friendships need not be confined to a single person, but may safely embrace all the wise and virtuous, with whom we have been long and intimately acquainted, and upon whose wisdom and virtue we can, upon that account, entirely depend.

(Incidentally, Smith also thought these people will be happy because they are content with themselves: 'A great part, perhaps the greatest part, of human happiness and misery arises from the view of our past conduct, and from the degree of approbation or disapprobation which we feel from the consideration of it'.)

Realpolitik

This is the high point in Smith's doctrine of friendship. However, it begs a question. What kinds of behaviour or virtues are thought praiseworthy, and who decides?

On the matter of who decides, Smith is clear that the answer is not moral theorists: whatever they say, they have little impact upon the actual behaviour of individuals. The best arbiter is the individual themselves, and the dialogue they have with their impartial spectator. Smith is in this way saved from a purely subjectivist theory of ethics: because they seek to be praiseworthy, the individual cannot simply justify their actions by saying that what they did seemed right to them; they must consider what society around them might consider to be right too.

But this still leaves the first issue as to what is praiseworthy. This is more difficult to answer. The problem is that commercial societies are pluralistic, so there is bound to be some debate as to the standards according to which individuals should behave. Take qualities like pride, ambition or obedience: one person's praiseworthy virtue is another's blameworthy vice. Not that Smith is alone in being vulnerable to such moral dilemmas. Deciding cases like these is a problem that any ethical theory has in the absence of moral absolutes. However, a more particular problem stems from the need Smith has for praiseworthiness to itself be thought praiseworthy. If commercial culture is confused about that too – compromising it in favour of utility, profit, exchange and so on – then his theory collapses. The shadowy observer dissipates, as it were, in the harsh winds of what people might call the real world – the realpolitik of commercial activity. People then inevitably return to seeking praise for its own sake.

It seems to me that this is just what happens at work. The determining utility of the workplace means that praiseworthiness is typically secondary to delivery. At work people are praised for the things they achieve: remuneration comes to those who impact the bottom line; people act out of utility – their 'role'. Even intangible qualities that might be thought praiseworthy, like entrepreneurialism or simple human pleasantness, must indirectly prove their worth in the workplace to be valued. Employment is not like school where people are rewarded for trying hard (fat cat CEOs may be an exception).

To put it another way, if few would challenge the idea that praiseworthiness is praiseworthy in theory, its value stands or falls on whether it is manifest in practice. If a commercial society – like a workplace – is one in which praiseworthiness is in fact a marginal concern, it seems that friendship will in turn struggle: people will on the whole be merely friendly with each other, rarely truly friends in the sense of loving someone for whom they are.

Hence, I think, the equivocation in Smith's notion of sympathy. It is as if he wants the affection that he sees in commercial society to be an expression of the full love of friends but when set against the conditions of the real world he can only make it stand up as a kind of decent fellow feeling.

Worse yet, there are other reasons to think not only that praiseworthiness flounders but also that friendship actually undermines social cooperation itself. Friends regard each other as special. They see each other as praiseworthy (or lovely) typically by way of a contrast with what they regard as unpraiseworthy (or unlovely) around them. Take a value like loyalty. Someone will value the loyalty of a friend because it appears to be absolute compared to the loyalty one might have, say, to a boss, which clearly has its limits.

From that it is only a short step to saying something else: if you are my loyal friend, then those others are not. Friendship, then, in practice may promote suspicion not cooperation. (There is also an argument that organisations are inherently suspicious of friendship since they set up networks of loyalties that can act against the organisation's best interests: the activities of friends can easily be viewed as time-wasting at best, or nepotistic and subversive behaviour at worst.)

So one is left with the feeling that although Adam Smith has high ideals for friendship, he is forced to settle for a lesser version of the virtue of social cooperation. In fact, the problem he has in reconciling friendship with commercialism is often exposed in the advice he offers elsewhere. For example, he can write that people should be 'capable of friendship' but avoid 'ardent attachments'. Or they should restrict their attendance at 'convivial societies' because they will interfere with the 'steadiness of industry'. Far from promoting friendship, commercial society as a whole seems to promote the personal ambiguities associated with utility-based friendship. At best, it is one of amicable strangers, or 'honorary friends' as the contemporary economist Paul Seabright has put it. But the quality of feeling that makes for truly good friendships would seem to be routinely under threat. Deeper friendships may form, but that is in spite of, not because of, commercialism.

Utility spreads

The suspicion that social cooperation values profit and politeness over praiseworthiness and knowing someone well was voiced by another eighteenth-century Scot. According to Adam Ferguson, commercial society is not merely indifferent to deeper friendships but positively cultivates enmity. This is because although it may promote interdependence, it does so at the price of substituting the virtues that would take care of others with those that take care of oneself. He painted a bleak picture of the market society he saw forming around him, 'dominated by a spirit of individualism, competition and legalism where relationships are defined and constrained by contracts and the profit motive'. He accused optimists like Smith of confusing virtue and utility: they would call a cow virtuous, he said, if it produced the right sort of milk. For Ferguson, the workplace is alienating, soul-destroying and isolating, playing to the worst detached and solitary instincts in human beings. In the market economy, man [sic] has therefore, 'found an object which sets him in competition with his fellow-creatures, and he deals with them as he does with his cattle and his soil, for the sake of the profits they bring'.

It should be said that the workplace and the culture of work that now exists within late capitalism has changed massively in the ensuing 250 years. Today, HR executives in progressive companies, for example, are seriously committed to moving away from command-and-control type management structures and increasing the choices employees have in the workplace. They want to make time for people in and around work, not only for chores that otherwise eat into their weekends, but also for activities that build praiseworthy aspects of character, from learning a language to taking a sabbatical. I recently heard the CEO of one multinational say that he refused to call his employees 'human assets', as the jargon dictates, since he did not own his staff but rather asked them for their time, if in return for certain rewards.

Alternatively, the male-dominated, heavy industry that characterised the industrial revolution of Adam Smith's time has largely collapsed in the West, and with it the grinding days that it demanded (though so too have the industrial communities that were arguably excellent environments for nurturing a sense of connection). Or one can point to the place and influence of women in the workplace that might promote a more humanly considerate environment.

However, these gains are themselves under threat – from utility again. Any positive effects are arguably being beaten back by the spread of flexible labour markets and the huge emphasis on productivity in the modern economy. This is nothing if not utility with a vengeance. Indeed, many fear that such a culture is deeper now than it was in Smith's day. Is not so-called vocational education little more than equipping people for greater productivity in the workplace?

The current predicament is well portrayed in Douglas Coupland's novel, *Microserfs*, the story of a group of friends working for Microsoft, the software giant. Dan, the narrator, describes how in the 1970s companies installed showers and sculptures in the workplace, 'to soothe the working soul'. This led in the 1980s to the blurring of the boundary between work and life. And now, inexorably completing the circle, people are asked to become their own corporations: 'Give us your entire life or we won't allow you to work on cool projects,' he says of Microsoft's attitude to its employees. Certainly, the number of hours people spend at work competes with time for friends elsewhere, to say nothing of what is owed to the family. This is doubly detrimental to friendship because apart from the adverse effects of time constraints, good friendships depend too on individuals nurturing a range of interests – a hinterland that modern work practices are quite possibly depleting.

In other words, the spectre of utility still haunts the workplace today. Whilst the poles may have shifted since Ferguson and Smith's day, there is little reason to think that the challenge posed by it is any less strong. Perhaps it is stronger because it is more insidious: if social cooperation in commercial society has mutated into social productivity under capitalism, our work culture is at least as indifferent towards friendship as ever it was.

2
Friends and Lovers

If you wanna be my lover, you gotta get with my friends.
                                                    The Spice Girls

The year is 1559 during the brief reign of Mary Queen of France, also
known as Queen of Scots. The scene is a festival in the renaissance
town of Bar-le-Duc. Two pairs of eyes meet across the crowd, a meeting
which one of them later described thus:

> We were seeking each other before we set eyes on each other, and at
> our first meeting, we discovered ourselves to be so seized by each
> other, so known to each other and so bound together that from
> then on none was so close as each was to the other.

A question: was this the start of an affair or a friendship?

Move forward, just over a hundred years, across the channel to
springtime in Deptford, South East London. A man and a woman are
in the grips of love, attested to by their prolific letters now in the
British Library. Their relationship began the year turbulently, but
Margaret is beginning to feel less anxious again for all John's intensity. She writes:

> What mean you to make me weep and break my heart by your love
> to me? Take me and all I have, give me but your love, my dear
> friend. Tuesday is longed for by me and nights and days move a
> tedious pace till I am near you.

A question: is it lovers or friends that will be reunited?

Now to the present day, to a crematorium in North London, and the end of a relationship. At the funeral, the man who survives recalls:

I was barely coherent, shaking violently through the music, trembling, wobbly-voiced, as I read the Maupassant, taking deep breaths to fight off tears: 'We must feel. That is everything. We must feel as a brute beast filled with nerves feels, and knows that it has felt and knows that each feeling shakes it like an earthquake. But we must not say that we have been so shaken. At the most we can let it be known to few people who will respect the confidence.'

The question again: does the man remember his lover or his friend?

The passion described in each case might suggest that these couples were lovers. They were, in fact, all friends. The first is Michel de Montaigne, the essayist and author of one of the most important philosophical pieces of writing on friendship, prompted by his relationship with Etienne La Boëtie. This exerpt, from that essay, describes their first meeting. The second comes from a letter of Margaret Godolphin, a maid of honour at the court of Charles II, who had a 'seraphic' friendship with John Evelyn, a friend of Samuel Pepys. The third comes from a book by the actor Simon Callow, entitled *Love Is Where It Falls: An Account of a Passionate Friendship*, a memoir of his relationship with the theatrical literary agent Peggy Ramsay.

And of what passion, for the fervent obsession within which each of these friendships flourished is arresting precisely because none of them was sexual. Montaigne and La Boëtie were both men and though same-sex relationships were a marginal concern of his, Montaigne thought them 'rightly abhorrent to our manners'. Of the second couple, one might easily come to the conclusion that they used Restoration religiosity as a cover for what would have been an affair, had Evelyn not been married. But that would be to misunderstand them: sex was never on the cards. It turns out that they enjoyed an intense friendship of a sort that had a long tradition up to the seventeenth century and is now largely forgotten. For Simon Callow and Peggy Ramsay the question of whether they would have a sexual relationship or not was relatively easily answered by numerous contingencies from Callow being gay to Ramsay being 40 years his senior. They excluded the possibility, though this is not to say that their relationship was not charged with erotic elements and troubled at times because of that. So, as so-called Platonic relationships, the friendships are intriguing because their passionate quality focuses us on a second set of ambiguities that can cause problems for friendship – now not revolving around the matter of utility but rather the question of sex.

Sex and friendship

This ambiguity is perhaps as familiar. At their best, sexual attraction and the feelings that exist between friends are both types of love. Sometimes, notably in the case of committed partners, this love shows itself as a happy synthesis of erotic and friendly affection. However, at other times, friendship and erotic love, whether or not actually expressed, form an unstable amalgam.

It may be that two friends come to sense a sexual undercurrent between them that far from sweeping them off their feet makes them feel decidedly uncomfortable and unsteady. In this case, we'd say that the question of whether or not to engage in an affair poses a threat to the friendship. Conversely, it may be that two lovers, brought together by a mutual sexual attraction, start to realise that there are no grounds for any long-term friendship between them, and as a result the relationship begins to fall apart. Now, it is friendship, or the paucity of it, that appears to question the basis of the sexual relationship. Alternatively, sex can hang a question mark over a friendship even when a physical relationship is barely thought of. For example, a man and woman may come to be friends at work and decide to go out for dinner together as an apparently natural extension of the friendship. Unwittingly, though, this seems to take them into uncharted waters as the sort of the thing that lovers, not friends, do. Again, the friendship flounders. Put more generally, cultural assumptions about the actions associated with a sexual relationship can imperil friendship as much as any actual erotic attraction itself (that Montaigne and La Boëtie, Evelyn and Godolphin, and Callow and Ramsay were able to overcome any such issues in their otherwise highly passionate friendships is what makes them so intriguing). There is, then, a play between sex and friendship that can be great, or conversely can complicate things terribly.

This is an issue that is arguably particularly critical today. The tectonic plates of marriage are shifting ground, giving rise to a new geography of the institution that is at least in part based on an idea of sexual friendship. Culturally, we see this reflected in many ways. One of the most obvious are sitcoms such as *Friends*, *Sex and the City* and *Will and Grace*. They thrive on the ambivalences of what the author Ethan Watters calls the 'tribe years' – the twenty- and thirtysomething years during which people remain unmarried and order their lives around long-standing friends instead. Thus the TV shows endlessly toy with their characters' sexual liaisons whilst keeping their friendships firmly centre stage. If and when the individuals do get married, or settle down, it is a sexual friendship that they will want. Alternatively, the tremendous success of *Bridget Jones' Diary* stems in large part from the seriousness with which the book explores modern friendship (and which, to my mind at least, the movies rather ruin because they focus too much on romance: the blunt and far more easily marketable question of sex – will they or won't they – has overridden the more subtle ambiguities of friendship).

Now, on one reading it may seem easy to untangle the ambiguities of sex and friendship. For example, it just seems ridiculous to suggest in some pop-Freudian kind of way that all friends of the opposite sex would go to bed with each other everything else being equal. The point was well made by the philosopher John Stuart Mill who had an intense and, before they married, controversial friendship with Harriet Taylor: 'We disdained, as every person not a slave of his animal appetites must do, the abject notion that the strongest and tenderest friendship cannot exist between man and woman without sensual relation.'

Alternatively, Freud had a point. The problem is not that the sex part always explicitly gets in the way, but rather that it might well hang a question mark over the friendship unconsciously or from time to time: there may always be a 'faint undercurrent of excitement' even between a St Francis and a St Clare. This erotic possibility, rather than a sexual inevitability, is no less powerful a manifestation of the possibly damaging play between sex and friendship.

(Another rather different way in which the question of sex might spoil friendship is in the realm of same-sex attractions. We will come to this in a later chapter but for now note that, in this case, the faint undercurrent does not need a boy and a girl to stir it up and, given that the fear of homosexuality can be as much of a threat as any actual homosexuality itself, even a suggestion of same-sex attraction is potentially enough to muddy the waters of friendship. This is not necessarily to impute everyone with some trace of gayness, like the suggestion that C. S. Lewis objects to so strongly in his essay on friendship, that 'the absence of smoke proves that the fire is very carefully hidden'. Rather, homosexuality complicates same-sex friendship primarily because of homophobia. This means that the very lack of sexual attraction needs to be demonstrated and made explicit. In other words, a fear of the gayness that may be taken as implied by a friendship between men, and I think it is fair to say that it is largely a male anxiety, can compel them to want to prove to the other, and to the outside world, that they are not homosexual – to the detriment of the friendship.)

Philosophically speaking, the sources of the confusion stem from the fact that erotic love and friendship are similar in certain respects, as well as being different in others. The similarities mean that people can easily, and happily, come to share the affections that are associated with both. The differences mean that less appropriate affections can then rise to the surface and generate the tension.

Similarities and difference

So consider, first, the ways in which erotic relationships and friendship are the same. For starters, both are excellent things to hope for, essential ingredients, we might say, for a life lived in all its fullness; love and friendship both call us into and become constitutive of our happiness. Alternatively, both counter the human condition of being incomplete and unfulfilled by ourselves, since alone we are not self-sufficient. What is more, whilst both stem from this need to be with others, both have the capacity to rise above the pure need of the individuals concerned too: a lover who wants sex and sex alone out of the relationship is usually thought exploitative, at least in time; someone who only wants friends for what they get out of them uses his friends in a pejorative sense and the friendship is sooner or later doomed. For similar reasons, both loves are implicitly or explicitly defined according to their ideal, though those ideals may be hard or impossible to achieve: even if we say such and such is in a manipulative relationship or has an exploitative friend, there is an implicit contrast drawn with what the relationship could be like at its best (someone will say, 'He only loved me for my money', thinking that love is so much more. Someone else will realise, 'She is only interested in me for what she can get out of me', implying that they hoped for so much more too).

Lovers and friends seem alike for what we might call technical reasons too. Both relationships are entered into voluntarily, unlike the relationship one has with country, class or family. Lovers and friends must both share a degree of trust, understanding and forbearance. Both loves can be jealous, one out of avarice, the other out of enmity. And both can operate apart from the law: sexual desire is antinomian, though various social institutions like marriage and taxation try to channel and control it; and friendship would, in E. M. Forster's famous phrase, betray country before it betrayed itself.

The other half of the story is the ways in which friendship and erotic love are different. For example, it might be said that friendship is calm, reasonable, harmonious and sober, whereas erotic love is spontaneous, irrational, wild and orgiastic. Or that friendship tends towards the mind, conversation and the spiritual, whereas erotic love is nothing without the body, touch and lust. Alternatively, friendship seems to develop over time: it loves to dwell on what has past and to ponder what is to come. But erotic love delights in immediacy; it exclaims, 'Now!'

Other differences apparently widen the gap. If friendship is not reciprocated it immediately loses its intensity and rapidly makes little sense: it is nonsense to say that someone is my friend but I am not their friend. Erotic love, in contrast can quicken regardless of whether the love is returned. Indeed, unrequited love produces eros' most exquisite passion – infatuation: a lover can love their beloved even in secret. Another difference concerns the relative ease with which friendships and lovers' relationships can be formed. Friendship seems easier, in the sense that most people would say they have many friends, notwithstanding the fact that they have only a limited number of good friends. At the same time, everyone knows the frustration of unattainable love, which suggests that whilst falling in love comes easily, being in a loving relationship does not.

Or again, once in a friendship, it seems reasonable to say that it generally brings out the best in people: friendly affection and moral behaviour appear to conspire together in a virtuous circle of love, since friends want the best for each other. The same does not necessarily follow in predominantly erotic relationships at all and it is easy to imagine all sorts of situations in which the purely erotic passion of lovers can descend into abuse, violence and hatred: a quarter of all murders are committed by a lover, far more than are committed by someone who was a friend. In summary it may seem that friendship tends to be reasonable, whereas erotic love is irrational; friendship warms to the mind, whereas sexual attraction wants the body; friendship must be reciprocated to make sense, love need not; and friendship is mostly virtuous, whereas eros can be murderous.

So one way of understanding how sex can hang a question mark over friendship, or vice versa, is to say that it happens when the similarities between the two loves are forced to stand uneasily alongside the differences. The issue is, once again, how to negotiate the ambiguous feelings that then arise. If a friendship is disturbed by undercurrents of sexuality – be that because of personal chemistry or an awareness of contravening social norms – what can be done about it? If the early days of a possessive sexual relationship are to evolve into the months and years of a more open and long-term sexual friendship, then how is it that eros' lion can be made to lie down with friendship's lamb? Even a happily committed couple will from time to time be aware of the conflict between the loves their relationship otherwise manages to synthesise: eros' possessiveness may sometimes be threatened by friendship's desire to welcome others in – as when one partner becomes good friends with someone else of the opposite sex; or friendship's reasonableness may still occasionally find eros' spontaneity irksome – at bedtime, for example, after a hard day's work.

It seems to me that sex can cause problems even in those friendships where the sexual element seems to be sublimated entirely, in a shared passion not so much for each other as for life itself. Eros is perhaps then like the sand in the oyster's shell. It is the grit around which a smooth, lustrous coating of friendship may form. But pearls have flaws and if they crack, the grit can be re-exposed.

These issues are not just philosophical ones, of course. More commonly, people will turn to psychology to get to grips with them. However, philosophy does have resources that perhaps shed a different, refreshing light on the matter. First, we will look at what Plato says on the matter, because he almost uniquely amongst philosophers has a theory of love that offers a path of reconciliation between sexual desire and friendship. Second, we will use Aristotle's thoughts again to consider how to negotiate the dynamics that arise out of the ambiguity of sexual and friendly feeling, that is to move along this path: in this respect, his ideas can be thought of as practical outworkings of Plato's theory. And third, we will turn to the case of passionate friendships – for it turns out, I think, that when passion, as opposed to erotic feeling, characterises a relationship, friendship is most able to flourish.

Immortal longings: a theory of love and friendship

Many modern philosophers fight shy of anything to do with sexual love. They may fear looking like the trendy vicar who gives sex talks based upon the biblical Song of Songs. They may worry about inadvertently divulging too much information, for, no matter how abstracted, thoughts on sexual matters are autobiographical to a higher degree than most: this kind of philosophy is done 'in the bedroom', as the Marquis de Sade delighted in endlessly repeating. However, it was not always like this. Ancient philosophers were intrepid, none more so than Plato.

In fact, the chaste phrase associated with his name – Platonic love – is actually a misnomer. His writing may try to guide an individual towards more spiritual longings but that is not to say Plato thought human beings were or should be free of physical desires. It is in his portrayal of Socrates that he works out what he thinks is the best attitude to have towards the starts, stirrings and satisfaction of eros. Indeed, Socrates, who was famous for claiming to know nothing for sure, made one exception to his wise ignorance: he was fully conversant with the wiles of erotic love. Moreover, I think Plato suggests that ultimately eros should lead to, though not necessarily be superseded by, friendship. How this might be possible is therefore of great interest in trying to unravel the harmony and discord that can be created by the interaction of these two loves.

A good place to start is at the point that Greek love seems such a problem for us today. The love that fascinated Plato the most, along with apparently many of his contemporaries, was the desire that can exist between a young man and a youth. It's a tricky area on a number of counts. Given that the homosexual element is not in itself thought illicit, it is, first, overwhelmingly male sexuality that Plato explores – that is, he appears to sideline anything that may be distinct in female desire. Second, there is the matter of the age difference between these Greek lovers and the concern to modern minds that their inherent inequality breeds abusive relationships. Third, there is the related anxiety over the criterion that the Greeks used to determine the ability to give consent – the appearance of a beard on the youth. We prefer the less ambiguous, and in practice more conservative, measure of age.

However, what is often overlooked is that ancient homosexuality worried Plato too, and for not dissimilar reasons. One of the places in which he raises the matter is in the *Symposium*. During Pausanius' speech, he argues that the reason why it is appropriate to love youths only after their beard has appeared is that it is only then that they can be thought to have developed a mind of their own, which means that the older partner will not be able to take advantage of the younger. In fact, Pausanius claims, with an optimism that would outdo most liberals, that the older partner will then want to share everything he has with his beloved and even spend the rest of his life with him. Moreover, he goes on to express the opinion that individuals whose urges lead them to seduce any boy, regardless of maturity, are debauched; every legal obstacle should be placed in their path. Not that this is any reason to ban homosexuality outright, for all the clarity of such a position: that would be both tyrannical and would foster a dull and stupid attitude towards sexual matters. Rather, he believes that the very complexity of the customs and conventions that govern homosexual behaviour is, in fact, their virtue. In other words, Plato saw perfectly clearly that sexuality is tricky. But the power of such feelings is no reason to don an emotional chastity belt. Rather, the trick is to steady yourself and take advantage of them, in a path that leads first to philosophy and then friendship. The question is how.

Plato's answer stems from a key insight. He thought that erotic love can lead to philosophy as much as the bedroom because both erotic love and philosophy – the love of wisdom – ultimately aim at the same thing, that is, immortality. To borrow a phrase of Oscar Wilde, lovers are in the gutter but they may also look to the stars. Strictly speaking of course, what is immortal is beyond the reach of human beings as mortal creatures. But tastes of immortality are possible, do in fact come in many shapes and guises, and it is these experiences that link eros to philosophy.

Consider one example, that of having children. According to another speaker in the *Symposium*, Diotima, parents have children not merely as a by-product of their sexual congress but because of this broader desire for immortality: if sex provides a taste of immortality because its 'petit mort' is ecstatic (literally, takes you out of yourself), children provide a deeper satisfaction of immortal longings because, in their offspring, parents live on.

Having said that, children are poor guarantors of such satisfaction since they rebel, change, and often died, at least until relatively recently. So, Diotima thought, individuals seek alternative intimations of immortality too. Achievement in sport and the accumulation of money are two: immortality here is sought in fame and fortune (which also explains why celebrity and money are sexy). However, they are fallible too, depending on various contingencies, not least pure luck.

Thus, Diotima suggests, the best way to gain as great a share in immortality as is humanly possible is philosophy – the pursuit of wisdom. Wisdom imparts the best sense of immortality since it is timeless, beautiful and true. A wise insight, she says, is like a child of the soul and it can never be lost. The seeker after wisdom is, therefore, very close to the passionate lover. (Or, as many teachers of adolescents know, knowledge is not just power, it is sexy too; it makes you seem like a god.)

Another way of understanding why erotic love is an excellent way into philosophy is to see that they are both, ultimately, concerned with the same things. Everyone falls in love and understands the lure of the beautiful, the other and the sense that love transforms and transcends the humdrum. And it is these same things – the beautiful and the good, the unknown and the other, change and transcendence – that are what matter to philosophers. Plato believes that love can make philosophers of us all.

He was not alone in thinking along these lines. Homosexual lovers, of the sort that Pausanias discussed, ideally were supposed not only to enjoy sexual passion but from that to develop a passion for things of the mind. Such an association between philosophy and eros was manifested in one of the best-known institutions of the ancient world, the gymnasium. This was both a sexually charged place for watching and being watched, and a key location for conversing, debate and instruction. To the ancient Greek mind, at least, the two things quite naturally went together.

When it comes to how these two elements might shape a relationship between a young man and a youth there is currently some debate amongst scholars. However, again the ideal would seem to be that the young man offers a mode of education to the younger – through talking with him, socialising with him, and introducing him to the virtues and vices of public life – attention that the youth should reciprocate with genuine pleasure and feeling, perhaps with, perhaps without, genital expression and/or everything that falls in between.

But falling in love is a complex, chaotic affair. It can lift the eyes to higher things, but it may equally prefer to dwell on things lower down. The beautiful body can come to dominate an individual's desire so completely that they have no energy left for philosophy. Plato understood this. It lay, I believe, at the heart of his worry about homosexuality. In short, he was faced with a dilemma. Whilst eros can lead to philosophy, eros in excess – infatuation – might just as easily eclipse any passion for wisdom, and smother the love that may be pregnant with insight. The question is how is it possible to love well and wisely?

This is where friendship comes in. Just how is revealed in another dialogue, the *Phaedrus*. The critical section comes in what is often called the Great Speech of Socrates. Here he describes the soul as divided into three parts, a charioteer pulled by two different horses. The first part of the soul is the charioteer, the voice of reason in the soul. The second part is one of the horses, which is powerful and obedient, driving the soul through life. The third part is the other horse, and it is wild, resisting the charioteer. All three parts of the soul are susceptible to love; in Plato's scheme the soul is, after all, that part of the individual which longs for heaven. But trouble arises because, when the soul sees a beautiful youth, his two horses pull against each other as the wild one rears up in the compulsive desire for sex. It is all that the charioteer, the voice of reason, can do to muster his strength and bring the wild horse under control.

This talk of heaven, chariots and wild horses is, of course, partly supposed to raise a smile. But the image of the charioteer reigning in the wild horse of erotic desire is one that clearly represents the frame of mind that Plato believes is necessary if someone is to love another well, and not merely give in to wanting to possess them. The implication is that it is only with some effort that it is possible to form relationships that are passionate but not so sexually excessive that the desire for philosophy is eclipsed.

However, if this is achieved then the couple concerned will develop a life together that is inspired by philosophy *and* friendship. Ideally, as Socrates puts it, it is a life 'of bliss and shared understanding'. In other words, not only do the erotic and philosophical elements come to resonate with each other but the two reach a shared understanding that is the basis of friendship, and a very great friendship at that.

Platonic friendship

'Love is the attempt to form a friendship inspired by beauty', was the Stoic expression. Socrates describes it in an appealing way too: he says the youth will be 'amazed by it as he realizes that all the friendship he has from his other friends and relatives put together is nothing compared to that of this friend who is inspired by a god'. This reference to a divinity is not merely a classical flourish. The god in question is eros, an acknowledgement that the two were originally drawn together by a sexual attraction. So what Socrates is arguing is that a friendship between lovers is not only possible but also can, via a mutual concern for the good things in life (that is, philosophy), make for one of the best kinds of friendship. This happens because the relationship comes to embody its passion in a certain way. The fervour and enthusiasm must not be primarily directed at each other, as was the case when they were new lovers, but should come to be directed towards the growing interests that emerge as the friendship does too. It is a passion for the things that the friends now enjoy together.

This movement from an erotic passion that focuses solely on an individual to a shared passion for life itself is well captured in an observation made by C. S. Lewis. He noted how lovers are typically depicted gazing into each others eyes, whereas friends portrayed together usually look straight ahead.

Nietzsche is another philosopher who pondered the move from lovers to friends. With Plato he saw it as something of a struggle. For example, in a deliberately provocative passage, he says that an obsessive love is actually the same as avarice (cupidity, we might say, noting the reference to the Roman god of love). It longs to possess the other at all costs:

> If one considers ... that to the lover himself the whole of the rest of the world appears indifferent, pale, and worthless, and he is prepared to make any sacrifice, to disturb any order, to subordinate all other interests – then one comes to feel genuine amazement that this wild avarice and injustice of sexual love has been glorified and deified so much in all ages ...

However, when lovers become friends a new passion becomes possible. Again Nietzsche does not pull his punches:

> Here and there on earth we may encounter a kind of continuation of love in which this possessive craving of two people for each other gives way to a new desire and lust for possession – a shared higher thirst for an ideal above them. But who knows such love? Who has experienced it? Its right name is friendship.

In summary: Plato's theory of love is that sexual attraction can, with a degree of will power, be channelled into a passion for things that the lovers share beyond (though not necessarily excluding) a desire for each other's bodies. This in turn makes way for a particularly wonderful kind of friendship. In a way, all Plato is doing is deepening the truism that a sexual relationship will only continue to grow if friendship feeds or even supplants the early physical attraction. One way of putting this is to say that lovers must learn to love each other body and soul if they are to stay together. But the Platonic, richer conception is to focus on the passion: when two individuals share a passion for life, erotic love and friendship find their best synthesis.

The next question to ask is how this theory of love can be brought to bear upon the ambiguous feelings that friends and lovers might share. This will come next in Aristotle's more practical reflections on love and friendship. But before that, briefly return to the problems that ancient Greek sexuality poses for us today.

We have, I think, covered the worry over its possibly exploitative nature: in Plato's case, at least, the ideal is reciprocal and mutual. However, there is still the matter of the exclusion of female desire. The first thing to say here is that there is clearly a large gap between social attitudes in fifth-century BC Athens and the twenty-first century, some of which are bridgeable and some of which are not. Along with slavery, the ancient Greek attitude towards women will tend to fall into the former camp whatever else is said. The question is whether Plato's ideas about sexual desire and friendship have anything to say to women today?

At one level, only individuals can answer that for themselves. However, there is evidence that Plato himself had women in mind when he wrote about love. For example, another speaker in the *Symposium*, Aristophanes, tells the story which the dialogue is possibly best remembered for: Aristophanes' myth. The story goes that originally human beings were two people in a single whole. Some were two men, some two women, some one man and one woman. The gods split human beings up as punishment for hubris and as a result human beings are condemned to spend their lives looking for their lost halves. It is a myth that neatly captures the power of the erotic drive. However, it also puts male and female desire on the same footing.

That Plato took female desire seriously is also revealed in his deployment of the female character Diotima. He puts into her mouth the fundamental insight that eros longs for immortality above all else. Quite why has puzzled many scholars. Some say that by making this heterodox move he signals the heterodoxy of his views. Others say that her femininity underlines the critical corollary to her insight which is that love's passion seeks to give birth to things other than itself – children and wisdom, fame and fortune, and of course, friendship. However, whilst Plato was no proto-feminist, I think we can also add that he wished to incorporate a sensitivity towards female desire in his theory of love, for all that it was bound to be framed in a discussion of male sexuality. That he comes to the conclusion that the best kinds of friendship are passionate, and not say comradely or competitive as a more masculinist account might conclude, certainly chimes with what many women write about female friendship to this day.

Practicalities

Aristotle was Plato's pupil, and he ventured into the same territory, taking a line which in certain respects can be thought of as building on that of his former teacher. He is never so explicit about sex, at least in his surviving writings: 'As for the pleasure of sex, no one could have any thoughts when enjoying *that'*, is one of his more memorable and faintly disparaging comments. However, if Plato has a theory as to how erotic love can lead to friendship, Aristotle is illuminating when it comes to the practicalities of the move.

In his *Nicomachean Ethics*, happiness is the chief concern. He assigns friendship top place in the hierarchy of happy-making relationships. However, friendly lovers, though lower down, can hope for some deep contentment too. In fact, according to Aristotle they can enjoy a sort of friendship even when their relationship is dominated by the sexual, inasmuch as both parties value the pleasures they receive from the other (this is actually a parallel point to the one that relationships based on utility can still be friendly too: the utility makes for friendship of sorts). He is quite clear, though, that this kind of happiness is compromised. Sexual pleasures vacillate (as utility comes and goes). What individuals find sexually attractive changes over time, as does the sexual appeal of their partner (and the two are usually out of sync). So, relationships with a heavy sexual component are fickle. The more the sex counts, the more broken hearts, affairs and infidelities accompany them.

For lovers not so obsessed, though, friendship can flourish. It is all a matter of overcoming the hurdles. For example, one problem Aristotle identifies is that relationships based predominantly upon sexual pleasures tend to form quickly (again, the same point as the speediness with which friendships based on utility form: they do so because they depend on things that are easy to share – that is, on things that do not necessarily demand much self-disclosure from the individuals themselves). As evidence, Aristotle cites young people who are particularly erotically inclined: 'hence they love and quickly stop loving, often changing in the course of the same day'. The problem with this is that their desire tends to colour their vision of everything else: their new-found lover looks uncompromisingly physically beautiful to them and appears beautiful in mind and spirit too. The danger, in turn, is that their vision becomes so clouded by swirls of emotion that they may in actuality know only very little about the person they claim to love. This illusion will fade sooner or later, and then the love needs to root itself more deeply in the beloved's true mental and spiritual character. Any potential for a long-term relationship rapidly disappears if nothing lovely is found there.

It is for this reason that when a love affair cools, the question of the lovers' future together is determined not by the intensity of their former passion, which may have been considerable, but by how deeply their passion has come to embrace the passion of friends; for it is as friends, not lovers, that they know each other truly.

At the same time, Aristotle continues, lovers like to spend time together and if they are interested in a long-term relationship, that is, in becoming friends, this is an advantage on which they can capitalize. Aristotle's advice is concise: choose the lover who you like the most, not only because the sex is great, but also because it is easy to spend time with them. Then you will get to know them – and they you. Any emerging friendship will shape the amorphous passions of romantic love and render it sustainable. What is more, it is possible to ascend a virtuous spiral in this process since if loving leads to knowing, knowing leads back to loving. So there is even a certain advantage that lovers have when it comes to achieving the things that are characteristic of best friendship: since the best sort of friendship necessitates knowing someone well, lovers are in a good position to do so since they spend so much time together.

This sense that friendship lies at the heart of what it is to truly love someone, and not sexual attraction, is, I think, what John Bayley, husband of Iris Murdoch, calls a sympathy of understanding. It is wholly different from 'that intoxicating sense of the strangeness of another being which accompanies the excitements of falling in love', as he puts it in his memoir of his wife, *Iris*. He notices that after the heat of their courtship, and in the earliest days of their marriage, something new emerged in their relationship.

> Already we were beginning that strange and beneficent process ... by which a couple can, in the words of A. D. Hope the Australian poet, 'move closer and closer apart'. That apartness is a part of the closeness, perhaps a recognition of it: certainly a pledge of complete understanding. There is nothing threatening or supervisory about such an understanding, nothing of what couples really mean when they say (or are alleged to say) to confidants or counsellors, 'the trouble is that my wife/husband doesn't understand me'. This usually means that the couple, or one of them, understands the other all too well, and doesn't rejoice in the experience.

This is a friendship that thrives on the subtle process of growing, mutual understanding. Thus many a couple will confess that with increasing years together the companionship, the shared life, is as important as the sex, or more so. Their physical intimacy comes to turn on intimate trivia as much as anything else, becoming partners who know a lot about each other's physical likes, dislikes, needs and pleasures.

Further, just because lovers become friends does not mean that their relationship will loose its passion. This is the very crux of the value of Plato's ideas about the friendship of lovers. It will include the humdrum, of course, for it is often on this level that friends like to share their lives together – 'some drink together, some play dice together, others train, or hunt, or philosophise together' was Aristotle's list of activities: it is at this level that friendship brings good and remedial things to life such as fun, wellbeing, satisfaction and companionship. However, inasmuch as their shared passion moves on from being focused exclusively on each other, so too the sexual element will evolve, becoming much more an expression of the friendship as opposed to pure eros, and friendship's intimacies, securities, commitments and ardour. The ecstasy will arise from what is known of the other rather than what is unknown. The sexual intimacy of eros becomes the embodied knowing of sexual friendship, which in turn becomes the physical and spiritual coexistence of partnership. Passion in this sense 'feeds back'. Thus, people say he or she has become more attractive to me now than ever.

Eventually sexuality ceases to be a threat to friendship altogether for the two loves learn to speak the same language. A synthesis of similarity and difference becomes possible: friendship speaks the language of the body as well as the mind, and sexuality becomes a manifestation of the friendship. Then the love called friendship need not think erotic love perilous. With passion widened, and the beloved well known, there is every reason to think that lovers might aspire to the best kind of friendships there are.

Better than sex?

Lucky lovers! But what of the case of friends who, although aware of a sexual frisson between them, resist the temptation, and never indulge it. And further, what of the passionate friendships for which there is no apparent desire to engage in any physical intimacy at all.

The latter case is easier to explain. In short, the erotic is spontaneously and uncomplicatedly sublimated in the friends' delight and enthusiasm for life together. Their passion exists only in the broader sense – Nietzsche's higher thirst or Plato's shared understanding. One can think of examples of this kind of friendship. It is what happens when philosophers or intellectual friends share a passion in their studies, reading, insights or wisdom; or when artists seek friends who are motivated by the desire to create something beautiful or expressive; or when friends who are interested in science together delight in the wonder of nature or noetic entities – strange as that may seem. Further friendships may well form between, say, a philosopher and an artist, or a scientist and a musician, or a gardener and an actor, since each recognises the passion that their friend has for something which, in turn, encourages and fuels their own interest. Even someone who has a passion for making money can find friends with a similar passion for power – say a politician.

I find my own connection with this chaste passionate potential in friendship when I think about the dynamic between myself and a friend, Guy Reid, who is a sculptor. He has a great gift for carving human figures in wood that have the uncanny appearance of being almost alive. When I first met Guy I found this ability of his quite intimidating since any creativity I possessed seemed woefully pedestrian in comparison. It was a privilege just to write an occasional press release for him when he was having a show. But as our friendship developed, I allowed myself to be inspired to pursue my own more creative hopes in writing. He awoke a passion in me. For example, I recall going to a literary festival to catch a whiff of the creative energy in writers I admired and at the festival being very conscious of my friendship with Guy. The friendship, I realised, was nurturing my desire to write.

When it comes to the case of friends struggling with sexual undercurrents in their relationship, the matter is, unsurprisingly, more complex. In fact, the question of sex may appear to hang in the balance almost indefinitely – even if the rational part of the individuals' minds knows that it will or should never happen. The complication that comes from such an unresolved sexual frisson is the suspense. Indeed, suspense is as much a cause of erotic frisson as any actual sexual attraction might be: people do not even need to fancy each other, just be conscious that they might; in Evelyn Waugh's phrase, even 'a thin bat's squeak of sexuality' can frighten people off or distract them from becoming friends. Further, people can misunderstand their feelings. In a culture in which sexual consummation is seen as the highest expression of love that two people can hope for, a fascination for someone is easy to mistake for falling in love, even when it is simultaneously obvious that a sexual relationship would be inappropriate, unsustainable and possibly ruinous of the friendship.

Of the three relationships with which this chapter opened, the friendship of Simon Callow and Peggy Ramsay was closest to this state of sexual possibility, at least when they first met. Callow has written about it honestly, insightfully and often colourfully in his book-length account of their friendship. It provides excellent material for philosophical reflection and a way of thinking through this set of sexual ambiguities.

In fact, for Callow and Ramsay it was not so much a bat's squeak of sexuality that they had to confront as the squawk of love at first sight.

At this first meeting we spurred each other on higher and higher with great thoughts and terrible truths until we finally fell silent, having completely exhausted ourselves. I got up to go and we shook hands, oddly, awkwardly. She sat at her desk, combing her hair and repairing her lipstick as I left the office. Going back through the reception area to pick up the script which I dimly remembered had been the occasion of my being there at all, I caught the eyes of the secretaries and blushed. It was as if Peggy and I had been making love.

Callow is, and was, well known as a gay man: when he met Ramsay he was in the middle of a love affair with a man called Aziz Yehia. However, partly because sexual orientation is rarely entirely clear cut, and partly because passion can be close to erotic feeling even in the most high-minded, the sexual suspense was still present between him and Ramsey, expressed in the passage above in the guise of the 'as if' they had been making love. This question had to be resolved if his friendship with Ramsay was to grow.

Callow describes the way the suspense was at least temporarily lifted a few days later as a result of Ramsay inviting him to an intimate, exotic dinner à deux. He reports how she shuddered when he kissed her on the cheek in greeting. She trembled when he said she was beautiful. She was, as Callow says, Tatiana receiving Onegin. But the bloody obvious was now clear even to our Tatiana; Callow did not desire her.

However, that was not the end of the story. The challenge now was to sustain 'that most beautiful and elusive thing, a passionate friendship'. At first, it did not look all that promising. Callow writes of a kind of uneasy ménage à trois that evolved: he loved Yehia and Yehia loved being loved by him; Ramsay loved Callow who in turn gained much from that love and returned it, though without consummation. But they survived a moment of truth, the first time they were all together, and after that Callow talks interestingly of how his friendship with Ramsay became more permanently established. They identified the areas they enjoyed talking about and educating each other on, notwithstanding the recognition that some things should be off limits. Later, for example, when they took to spending evenings together listening to records, he writes:

> Sometimes, as we listened, we would hold hands, but that was a little too explicit. Generally we sat in separate pools of emotion, as if contemplating some grief that was beyond physical or verbal expression, a grief that we both knew about but could not name.

What is arresting about those evenings is that although they did not touch, their mutual separateness was not experienced as aloneness but as the deepest moments of friendship. Callow later recalls that those evenings were among the best evenings of his life.

How can we describe this friendship? Some might be tempted to say that the boundaries they had to enforce were the product of unresolved sexual tensions that persisted between them; their relationship was irreconcilably ambiguous, as if they were like tempestuous lovers endlessly delaying gratification, swinging from one emotion to the next but never finding a centre. But I think that Callow and Ramsay's friendship is much more than that. If, for example, they had been unable to redirect their passion to anything other than an unhealthy absorption with each other, Ramsay would not have awakened in Callow a talent that he now confesses to valuing even more than his acting, that of writing. He dedicates his first book to her as a monument to their friendship.

This is a crucial clue for understanding the thing that happened between them and is another example of the redirection of passion Plato identifies. Like a painting, that works with the mean materials of canvass and oil to conjure up a world that barely existed before, their friendship transformed the dollops of colourful passion which were given to them upon first meeting and which might have been merely thrown together in an affair, so that with a kind of discipline and restraint, as well as a joyful enthusiasm, they could rework them into a life on an altogether higher plane. The celibacy that this involved is not supposed to evoke a prohibition or a stigmatisation of sexuality. Rather it is to point to a voluntary renunciation that emerges from within a relationship when friends of this sort sense that self-control in one area will make for a transformation of themselves as a whole.

Friends like Callow and Ramsay have distinguished, and discarded, a possible physical response from a love of the other person's intellect, creativity or soul. They do not seek a desire for close physical intimacy – though they simultaneously do not compromise the passion that makes for their friendship

A further example of how this can come about, and this time in a case when an affair was certainly on the cards, is beautifully portrayed in Sofia Coppola's film, *Lost in Translation*. Bill Murray plays Bob Harris, an old movie star, who when in Tokyo on a mindless trip to endorse a brand of whiskey, meets Charlotte, played by Scarlett Johansson, who is similarly stranded in the city while her husband, a photographer, does a shoot. The story is of their encounter, and what is striking is that whilst there is an erotic charge between the two from the start they do not embark upon an affair. Part of the film's brilliance stems from the way it toys with the audience's Hollywood assumptions that they will, whilst simultaneously conveying the sense that something would be lost if they did. That something is the passion they have for their own lives. To become lovers would have been to lose that passion, and the chance to quicken it, in the loss of self that a sexual encounter would revel in. Friendship, in contrast, gave them the gift of being able to return to their lives with a sense of new possibility.

Getting with friends

Callow's story raises a final set of complications that we have only skated over thus far, that of the ménage à trois of two lovers and a friend. The complexity here arises when a new lover finds an old friend threatening, or in Callow's case when a new friend troubles an old lover. Is it possible to have one person who is your committed lover and another who is your close friend? And what of the relationship between those two individuals, for is there not the possibility of threat again, should the lover ask what the friend gives that they cannot?

In such love triangles, those who suddenly find themselves playing third fiddle may find it difficult to deal with the intimacy of the other two. Unsurprisingly, then, Callow's partner Yehia was intimidated by Ramsay. Callow writes when all three met together:

> It could have been the end of a number of things: my friendship with Peggy, but also, to my amazement, it seemed to threaten the continuation of my relationship with Aziz. Next to Peggy, everyone seemed less: less passionate, less perceptive, less brilliant, less honest, less absolute. And Aziz had seen, not only how important

Peggy was in my life, but a side of me, fervent and wild, which was only brought forth by Peggy.

What Callow sensed was that his friendship with Ramsay somehow threatened his lover because his relationship with Ramsay was, in the chaste sense, more passionate. Clearly, on one level, the resultant sense of threat was groundless. Sexually speaking, Yehia had no competition in Callow's eyes. But Ramsay was a threat not because she might have become Callow's lover; that faint possibility had been pushed aside. Rather, the problem was that her passionate hold over him challenged the ideal of romantic love that was part of Callow and Yehia's relationship.

This, then, is the nub of the final issue to do with friends and lovers. In today's world, there is a myth of romantic love based upon the idea that two lovers become one flesh, a totalisation of life in the other, supremely enacted in sexual ecstasy which is symbolic of that union. The myth or ideal tends to exclude others, not because lovers do not want friends, but because it tells them that their friends are incidental – pleasant but non-essential adornments to the lover's life together. Although few people in real life believe the myth in its entirety, it is difficult to ignore entirely too. Thus, Yehia could not ignore the fact that Ramsay was essential to awakening Callow's passion for life, and this seemed to contravene the romantic awakening that 'should' have been exclusive to their relationship. It was as if there was a third person in the marriage; hence the sense of threat.

It is indeed a brave soul who would come between lovers. Think of the estrangement that can come about between friends after one of them marries. Or just how hard it can be to sustain a friendship when one friend starts a new, sexual relationship. (Though this is not to say that lovers cannot in time find a certain release in encouraging their partners' friendships. That happens precisely for the reason that when a partner's eyes periodically turn from the lover back to an old friend it provides the lover with a break from the burden of the romantic myth, with its almost dictatorial insistence on total, exclusive involvement.)

Perhaps friendship should assert itself more strongly. It might refuse the otherwise overwhelming force of romantic love to declare the joys of its own passion, though that is a hard thing to do in a culture besotted with the power of possessive obsession. But the thought provides us with a good point of conclusion. For contra the myth, there is a love that does not desire to possess. It is called friendship. When friendship is the determining force in a relationship, individuals are able to find themselves and a passion for life, not merely lose themselves in love.

3
Faking It

Most friendship is feigning.
William Shakespeare

The best of friends can be found in the most unlikely of places. Few would associate Friedrich Nietzsche with friendship, for example. In the popular imagination this nineteenth-century philosopher is 'depressing'; he spoke in the language of fire and ice, proclaimed the death of God and created the character of Zarathustra who wanders alone in mountains and deserts. If people know anything of his life it might be that he fell out with his sometime mentor and friend Richard Wagner (the split was of operatic proportions). So to most, including those philosophers who have studied his work, he is not readily associated with the affectionate spirit of amity.

But contrast that image with this reality. On 19 November 1877 he wrote this to Paul Rée another philosopher:

> In my entire life I have not had as much pleasure as through our friendship during this year, not to speak of what I have learnt from you. When I hear of your studies, my mouth waters with the anticipation of your company; we have been created for an understanding of one another.

Alternatively, on 22 January 1875 he wrote to his sister Elizabeth:

> It is precisely we solitary ones that require love and companions in whose presence we may be open and simple, and the eternal struggle of silence and dissimulation can cease. Yes, I am glad that I can

be myself, openly and honestly with you, for you are such a good friend and companion.

Even in the case of Wagner for whom his antagonism was real, Nietzsche acknowledged his continuing debt to his former friend throughout his life.

Private lives do not automatically translate into public philosophy but Nietzsche also devoted several thousand words to the subject of friendship in the books of his so-called middle period, words which because of his aphoristic style pack a punch that the word count alone only hints at. His deep concern with the nature of friendship during this time was undoubtedly connected to the struggles he was having with Wagner as much as the strength of the friendships that he shared with others. So the details of the friendship and then the split perhaps provide an illuminating introduction to his thoughts on the matter.

They had met in 1868 and within 12 months he was a close friend of both Wagner and his mistress Cosima, the daughter of Liszt, visiting them frequently on Lake Lucerne. Their affection revolved around their admiration for Wagner's music (Wagner was not given to modesty where greatness was concerned) and their enthusiasm for the philosopher Schopenhauer. This infamous philosophical pessimist believed that the world was an illusion, the emanation of a daemonic will. The way people commonly experience the will is sexually, a yearning which, Schopenhauer thought, inevitably leads to suppurating frustration or rank satiation. Not the best grounds for human happiness and friendship there one would have thought, though his ideas achieved great popularity at the time. The reason Wagner and Nietzsche liked him was that he thought art was the only way out of the will's bind because only the aesthetic is disinterested or 'unwilful', supremely so in the case of music which provides a particularly direct means of transcending the human animalistic lot. Wagner opened Nietzsche's mind to the possibility of that transcendence. And the depth of feeling and debt that Nietzsche owed him in this period of his early development is shown in his book of the time, *The Birth of Tragedy*. It begins with nothing less than a 'Preface to Wagner' and includes material he had presented at Cosima's 33rd birthday celebration.

However, only a handful of years later in what we now know as his middle period, Nietzsche had shifted. The transitional book is *Untimely Meditations*. It includes another chapter on Wagner, entitled 'Richard Wagner in Bayreuth', but is now interesting because, as many

Nietzschean scholars note, the piece is the only occasion on which Nietzsche's work exhibits a conflict of sincerity; he was moving on but could not yet leave Wagner behind.

The moment for a clean break came in 1876 at the first Bayreuth Festival. Nietzsche was apparently revolted by the philistine crowds that he thought Wagner wooed merely in order to pay the bills, and he fled to the countryside with blinding headaches (he may also by this stage have looked at his Schopenhauer again: the one exception to Schopenhauer's love of music was grand opera which he thought an unmusical invention for unmusical minds). However, this histrionic revulsion does not feel quite reason enough for a permanent break. It is as if Nietzsche used his disapproval of Bayreuth as an excuse for it. The question is why?

Petty factors, such as the extent to which Wagner's brilliance eclipsed Nietzsche's rather pathetic abilities as a composer, could also have come to a head, though these animosities again do not feel reason enough and cannot have been the whole story. Wagner, for example, was not aware of the rift for some time and when Nietzsche later offered another reason, that the cause had been his horror at Wagner's conversion to Christianity, that does not ring true either: Wagner's Christianity had been in evidence since at least 1869. It seems that Nietzsche had come to the realisation that he had to remove himself from Wagner's sphere of influence if he was to make anything of his own life and that meant he had to manufacture a break, at least in his own mind. In other words, it was not that he came simply to loathe Wagner and everything he stood for, though he did represent a way of life that Nietzsche now wanted to critique strongly. It was that Nietzsche recognised the deep impact Wagner's friendship had had on him and would have continued to have had, so that, like a child who must violently leave the womb to be born, he too had not only to turn his back on Wagner but cut the cord as well. Paradoxically, and consciously or not, his break was out of a respect for the power of profound friendship.

It is easy to see Nietzsche exploring the echoes of this complex matter in subsequent reflections. Though they are not straight-forwardly autobiographical, he writes:

> The friend whose hopes one cannot satisfy one would rather have for an enemy.

And,

> If we have greatly transformed ourselves, those friends of ours who have not been transformed become like ghosts of our past: their

voice comes across to us like the voice of a shade – as though we were hearing ourself, only younger, more severe, less mature.

Or,

Just as in order to walk beside an abyss or cross a deep stream by a plank one needs a railing, not so as to hold on to it – for it would at once collapse if one did that – but to give the eye a feeling of security, so as a youth one has need of people who without knowing it perform for us the service of a railing. It is true that, if we were really in great danger, they would not help us if we sought to rely on them, but they give us the quieting sensation that there is protection close at hand (for example fathers, teachers, friends, as all three usually are).

Conversely, perhaps he feared developing a habit in relation to Wagner that he saw in other people who disparage and diminish those that they know in order to maintain their own sense of self-respect:

Many people mistreat even their friends out of vanity when there are witnesses present to whom they want to demonstrate their superiority: and others exaggerate the worth of their foes so as to be able to show with pride that they are worthy of such foes.

Another longer paragraph extends the theme and also suggests a framework within which to flesh out Nietzsche's wider understanding of friendship. He observes that amongst people who have a gift for friendship (note: 'have a gift' – these are not people who are simply bad at friendship), two types predominate. One type of person is like ladders; the other type is like circles. Ladder-types are individuals who are in a continual state of ascent in life. Life for them is a journey of change, evolution and progress. At each stage of their development, these people find friends who aid and encourage them and who in turn they aid and encourage. One can imagine, say, the life of a politician whose career is dotted with such friendships. At college they hang out with malcontents who inspire them. During their twenties they are nurtured by mentors who discipline them. In their prime they befriend individuals who are interested in the machinations of power, the power that they want to exercise at this point in their careers too. And then, in their dotage and disillusioned with power, they reflect on the vanities of life with those who are wiser and less sure.

The trouble that ladder-types find with friendship is that through no fault of their own this succession of friends rarely get on with each other. The malcontents will despise the mentor who will envy the powerful who will be irritated by the wise. So, passing friendships are a consequence of the ladder-life that the individual leads; later phases of development inevitably abolish or infringe upon the earlier. Therefore, the ladder-type has a philosophy of friendship which says that it is a mistake to expect or to try to cultivate close, life-long relationships. Harmony is sacrificed on the altar of progress.

The second type of individual who is good at friendship, the circle-like, also draws individuals with different characters, dispositions and talents around them but in a way that diffuses any awkwardness or antagonism. Typical of such a person might be a celebrity who counts their management, their peers, their family and even some fans as friends. Their charisma or personality provides a focus for the circle of friends which blurs the differences between them and keeps them friendly over long periods of time. To be a friend with the circle-type is like being friends with the host of a party who oils the wheels of communication with champagne and charm.

Nietzsche clearly thought of himself as a ladder-type. The implication of the analogy is that not only do circle-types compromise themselves by being all things to all people but also their friendships tend to be shallower too. This is an important point. In Nietzsche's book, longevity is not the determining measure of friendship. There is nothing wrong with long-lived friends per se: it is rather that time can take the dynamism out of friendship. Friendships that have gone on for too long become idle. The individuals then do not have enough to do with each other and wind away the hours talking about this and that, conspiring in indecision and perhaps in all honesty becoming nuisances to one another. 'It is prudent to form friendships only with the industrious,' Nietzsche concludes. He also suspects that such relationships are untrustworthy because when the bottom falls out of the friendship but the former friends cannot quite bring it to an end, they constantly strive to re-establish their intimacy with each other, as sure a sign as there is that habit has taken over real affection or closeness.

Incidentally, this observation about the need for dynamism in good friendship is a useful point since it is a dimension that is often forgotten. This has, no doubt, something to do with the fact that a surprising number of philosophers reflect on friendship after the death of a friend. Montaigne wrote his essay after La Boëtie had died. Cicero's dialogue on friendship remembers a friend too and opens with a discussion of mourning. Augustine's most heartfelt thoughts on friendship similarly stem from the pain of a death. The reason for this is presumably that untimely death tends to lead to the understandable desire to eulogise, though it also has the effect of preserving the friendship in its highest moment. If Montaigne's, Cicero's or Augustine's friend had lived on, their ladder-like lives would probably have separated them from the friends they remember; and if that had happened they might well have thought less of the friendship as a result. In contrast, Nietzsche can inject this dynamic of personal development or overcoming into the concept of friendship by refusing to hold onto great friends simply for sentiment's or loyalty's sake.

Truth hurts

At the same time, even ladder-types like to have circles of friends around them, and for the same reason that most people say, or like to say, that they have wide circles of friends. They figure that with most people it is better to be friendly even when you feel otherwise because, first, at a day-to-day level, it makes for a happier life, and, second, because to expose every friendship to the full force and struggle of personal change would be asking too much. Again, here is the paradox exhibited in Nietzsche's break with Wagner: only friends who have at one time identified closely may at a later time come to a definitive split. Mere friends will merely drift apart. Or, to put it another way, if someone who you know only slightly offloads the secrets of their heart to you, you quickly sense its inappropriateness. 'I hardly know them!', you will protest to a better friend.

But there is a price attached to having wide circles of friends, one which opens up the third set of amity's ambiguities. They are the ambiguities of closeness and distance (what is appropriate and how do you redress the balance when someone 'invades your space'); honesty and dissimulation (how truthful can you be with a particular friend or is it often better to obfuscate, or even tell a small fib); and loyalty and the need, sometimes, to make a break. In fact, when you start to look, it quickly becomes apparent that in a million little ways, as well as some large ones, friendship is often a matter of nothing less than faking it. Or, to use Shakespeare's phrase, most friendship is feigning.

In saying this, I am not talking about the ways in which people emote and just blatantly lie in the *name* of friendship. The faux-friendliness of the call centre, the salesman and the chat show host is as nauseating or amusing as it is transparent. Rather I am talking about people who would count themselves as friends to greater or lesser degrees but nonetheless employ what might be called the 'kind vices' of half-truth, evasion, prevarication and pretence. The point is that they sense that the friendship would not bear the weight of the whole truth of what could be said. If that were voiced, 'the pebbles [would be] set rolling, the friendship would follow after, and fall apart', as Nietzsche put it.

The examples of such behaviour are legion. Someone smiles rather than admit their malign thoughts about their best friend's new boyfriend. They scream inside rather than speak out on the disciplining of their friends' children. They conveniently forget the suggestion of holidaying, realising that to go away together would be a whole different ballgame to merely having dinner every other week. Alternatively, people can behave almost as if they were different persons with different friends, a schizophrenia that provokes great anxiety at the thought of, say, a birthday party at which everyone comes together. Then there is the competitive element to negotiate. If everyone confessed like Gore Vidal that 'whenever a friend succeeds, a little something in me dies', friendship would soon die too.

Friends are also complicit in each others' feigning for fear, in Shakespeare's phrase, of appearing 'unlearned in the world's false subtleties'. Celebrities, again, are past masters at this. A newspaper profile of Donatella Versace noted that her room was littered with signed pictures of her famous friends: a silver-framed photograph of Catherine Zeta-Jones clutching her Oscar in a black Versace dress had written across it, 'Dearest Donatella, a friend to cherish, I love you, Catherine' and was next to a signed picture of Madonna and her children (though much to her credit Donatella protested that her real friends in her real life were not famous. 'I go to parties for work,' she retorted).

Nietzsche records friendship's feigning foibles in a series of aphorisms and comments that are sharp, often playful and should perhaps be read as if uttered by Woody Allen, excusing the Germanic constructions.

In many people, the gift of having good friends is much greater than the gift of being a good friend.

One should not talk about one's friends: otherwise one will talk away the feeling of friendship.

The man had the great works but his companion had the great faith in these works. They were inseparable: but it was obvious that the former depended wholly on the latter.

They were friends and have ceased to be, and they both severed their friendship at the same time: the one because he thought himself too much misunderstood, the other because he thought himself understood too well – and both were deceiving themselves! – for neither understood himself well enough.

All this is the art of friendship and a fine art it is too. Its method is propriety. Its medium is often gossip, because what is not spoken to one friend is usually whispered to another ('There will be few who, when they are in want of matter for conversation, do not reveal the more secret affairs of their friends,' wrote Nietzsche. 'Life is not worth living unless one can be indiscrete to intimate friends,' was how the intellectual Isaiah Berlin expressed it). Its message is, 'I know you know but we both know not to go there'. Incidentally this is why I think electronic forms of communication are so risky for friendship. It is often said that email, texting, telephones and online video are good for modern human relationships since they can cope with separation and the pace of life, and allow people to be friends with many others. What is forgotten is that there is no substitute for face-time. This is not just because the quality of communication counts more than the quantity of communications in friendship. It is also because it is only when you are in someone's presence that you can receive all the signals, read all the nuances and rise to the demands of the game. Communication technologies are blunt instruments that may easily wound with the misunderstood word or sign, a wound that can fester if the memory of physical proximity is running low. The risk is even greater for those who think they can foster a friendship solely via a mobile display or PC screen. Screens screen. What has been missed or misread is highly likely to check or undo any nascent affection.

What are we to make of this plethora of dissimulation? In short, both little and a lot. Nietzsche again helps. He did not give the lie to friendship to disparage it. Rather, he understood that for the most part friendship is human, all too human. For this reason a degree of dissimulation is required on occasion in even the closest of friendships.

There was a time in our lives when we were so close that nothing seemed to obstruct our friendship and brotherhood, and only a small footbridge separated us. Just as you were about to step on it, I asked you: 'Do you want to cross the footbridge to me?' – Immediately, you did not want to any more; and when I asked you again, you remained silent. Since then mountains and torrential rivers and whatever separates and alienates have been cast between us, and even if we wanted to get together, we couldn't. But when you now think of that little footbridge, words fail you and you sob and marvel.

There is no such thing as *merely* picking the right moment. If too much is said the consequences for the vast majority of friends, and perhaps every friendship at least some of the time, are serious. So with regards to the dissimulation, one should make little of it, in the sense that one should carry on as usual with one's friends, and much of it, in the sense that to try to be more *openly* honest will for the most part be disastrous.

But this does not mean that one cannot ask the question why? The fundamental problem is twofold. First, even if we think we know someone well, our judgements about them are usually at least a little off the mark and so would warrant their vexation were they made known; it is better to avoid offence by forming little habits of evasion. Second, and more profoundly, people do not on the whole know themselves very well either. Nietzsche deploys an analogy of the self as a castle to describe this, a building that is both a fortress and a prison. Inside it is dark, full of shadowy corners and echoing chambers, though it also has windows out of which the individual gazes. The windows do allow the individual to see beyond themselves, perhaps to another guarded self. But what they show up most of all are the barriers and defences that people construct around themselves. 'Man [*sic*] is very well defended against himself, against being reconnoitred and besieged by himself, he is usually able to perceive of himself only his outer walls.' The reason people live in castles – that is, choose to know little about themselves – is because having the dark corridors of the mind brought into the light of day is not very pleasant. It is much more preferable to see oneself in gently distorting mirrors than to know oneself very well. To put it another way, if we feign friendship with others, to cover up what we think of as their faults, we will perhaps even more readily feign friendship with ourselves. The tough question that someone might ask of their friend – would they be our friend if they knew us well? – is also a question we can ask of ourselves; would we be our friend if we knew ourselves well? Thus, in the million little ways to themselves as well as others, friends reach for the mask and the world is a friendlier place for it:

Through knowing ourselves, and regarding our own nature as a moving sphere of moods and opinions, and thus learning to despise ourselves a little, we restore to our proper equilibrium with others. It is true we have good reason to think little of each of our acquaintances, even the greatest of them; but equally good reason to direct this feeling back on to ourself. And so, since we can endure ourself, let us also endure other people.

Another self

But is the price we pay for wider circles of friends invariably that of having to endure ourselves and others, at least on occasion? Is the well meant but feigning goodwill we show others mostly little more than an implicit acknowledgement that we are not very nice people and, for at least some of the time, our friends are not very nice too? The answer may be yes. But this negative image covers a more positive possibility. For sometimes toleration and dissimulation can give way to truthfulness and personal insight. It may only be achievable with one or two friends between whom a profound trust exists, or it may only come about a handful of times in life when the moment is right. But when it does, friends can rise above the ambiguities of everyday interactions and enter a zone in which they speak to each other truthfully and directly as another self. To this matter we now turn.

The notion that the closest kind of friend is one who is another self is deployed by nearly all the philosophers of friendship. However, it can be meant in several different ways. It is never meant solely in the trivial sense that friends share similar interests or pleasures, though friends may clearly both delight in football, fashion or food. Some philosophers use it in a romantic sense; the friend as another self implies that friends almost become one person, 'one soul in two bodies', as Montaigne put it. Nietzsche, though, objected to this emphasis. He did not want to 'confound the I and Thou'. For him, 'another self' must also carry the implication that friends are still 'other' to each other too. So, the friend who is 'an other self' is rather someone with whom individual goals, personal aspirations and private hopes coincide – at certain moments or over periods of time. The joy of the friendship is not the collapse of all boundaries between the individuals. Neither is it a like-mindedness that any group of people might feel. Rather, it is the realisation that they are headed in the same direction. They are friends, as Ralph Emerson put it, who exclaim to each other: 'Do you see the same truth?' – first with surprise and then with delight. This connection becomes more than a happy coincidence or pleasant discovery but a great blessing. 'In loving their friend they love what is good for themselves,' Aristotle said. 'For the good person, in becoming a friend, becomes a good for the person to whom they become a friend.'

This is a subtle point which is worth dwelling upon and has unexpected consequences, not least of which is that the best of friends may be found in the most unlikely of places. The point is well illustrated in the story told in the Oscar-winning movie, *Gods and Monsters*, directed by Bill Condon. It relates the last days of the life of the Hollywood director James Whale, played by Ian McKellan, whose fame and fortune was made with his film *Frankenstein*. Long after, in his declining years, Whale formed a friendship with his gardener, Clayton Boone, played by Brendan Fraser. This set tongues wagging in Tinseltown since Whale was a known homosexual, a fact to which the heterosexual redneck Boone was at first oblivious, then horrified, and only latterly indifferent. It is that transformation which was the key to a relationship that led to the discovery of a most unlikely and penetratingly honest friendship.

In the movie, the relationship begins unpromisingly when Whale asks Boone to sit for him under the ruse that Boone has an artistically fascinating face. It is a gratuitous come-on though it provokes Boone into reflecting a little on himself and his life. Something deeper between them begins to emerge when, at a second sitting, they realise that, for all their differences, they have something in common; they are both originally from poor families. Whale has kept this hidden from his starry Hollywood 'friends', a dissimulation that he is awakened to in the openness of Boone's face 'that makes me want to tell the truth'. Trust grows, and they confess their greatest secrets to each other: Whale relives the painful story of the great love of his life and Boone reveals his shame that he never saw action as a Marine. This latter revelation is important not only because of the confession itself but also because up to that point Boone thinks that, unlike Whale, he has no interesting stories to tell about his life and indeed could not even tell them if he had. That is a very good story, Whale says tenderly, one to match his own. Their relationship has become a friendship because in the telling of stories they not only find an equal and mutual respect for each other – many friendships get there – but because they have been able to be completely honest with one another.

In the final scenes, the film cuts to several years later. Boone is watching a repeat of one of the Frankenstein movies on television with his son and he remembers his friendship with Whale. The monster is heard wailing, 'Alone bad. Friend good.' The movie ends, and Boone shows his son a pencil sketch which Whale made of his original idea for Frankenstein, saying that he knew the man who made the movie. On the back is written, 'For Clayton, friend?' (the question mark is wonderfully indicative of the ambiguity of honest friendship). His son retorts, 'Is that just another one of your stories, Dad?' It highlights the legacy of Whale's friendship and the good thing which now characterizes his relationship with his son. Boone has overcome the limitations of his origins in a new ability with and love of stories.

This, then, is the way that a friend can be said to be another self; they nurture what we might think of as a side we never knew we had. It is in such friendship that people find the courage and humility to overcome the stalemate of the little lies or ignorances in which most friendships trade, and turn to work on themselves and achieve the good things which as individuals might be beyond them. Is it not the rare, close friend who shares the intimacy of faults that can speak gently and with precision to our own? (Incidentally, it is far from clear that a partner is always the best person to impart such truths; though lovers may devise their own means of speaking honestly to one another!)

The story of Whale and Boone's friendship illustrates two further paradoxes in this friendship of another self. First, it is the difference that eventually counts – what is unknown or unsettling – rather than the safe, familiar similarity that typically brings people together. What is strange challenges the friends to widen their horizons, search their souls and strive to speak honestly. 'It is not in how one soul approaches another but in how it distances itself from it that I recognise their affinity and relatedness,' says Nietzsche. Second, if the key to this kind of friendship is its challenge, its honesty can also be uncomfortable. To bear such frankness requires the right combination of timing and humility. (In fact, in Whale and Boone's case, Whale comes to see his predicament as a lonely old man perhaps too clearly for, though there is a certain catharsis in the act, he ends up killing himself.) This is why this kind of friendship is relatively rare and most of the time friends opt for at least a degree of feigning. In fact, Nietzsche provocatively suggests that someone who seeks such an appraisal from their friends might do better to turn to their foes, since enemies have the virtue of being honest and not counting the cost. Foes as friends in any literal sense is, of course, nonsense. But when the ultimate test of friendship is the ability to challenge one another, someone who might for a while be regarded as a bad friend could prove themselves a good friend in the longer term. Like a difficult book, the difficult friend may teach us something; affront at an initial presumption of unfriendliness may turn into gratitude for speaking the truth over time. Discernment is key. Someone who is simply evil or unjust, impulsive or unsteady, will never be a good friend.

Nietzsche is not the only philosopher to have thought that such genuinely challenging friendships are scarce and that the moments of truth they offer are fleeting in any individual's life. According to Plato, Socrates was aware of it too. In his dialogue on friendship, the *Lysis*, Socrates not only concludes that he and his interlocutors have not been able to discover what friendship really is but also he confesses to wanting a true friend more than anything else. The reason Socrates doubts whether he will ever find such a friend stems from his life as a philosopher. When he was young, the oracle at Delphi had told him that no-one was wiser than he. This idea frightened him and so he took to wandering the streets of Athens in search of someone who would prove the oracle wrong. He was not able to. What is more his conversations with people increasingly revealed how little he knew. As a result he came to the conclusion that what the oracle must have meant was that no-one else realised as profoundly as he did how little they knew. His wisdom was being wise to his ignorance. This left him in a quandary with regards to friendship. On the one hand, he could not shake off a lingering sense of loneliness because no-one he met shared this profound sense of ignorance in the way he did and so could be another self to him. On the other hand, talking to people all day long meant that he enjoyed wide circles of (admittedly) lesser types of friends. This is the paradox of putting a high value of honesty on friendship. Many people one meets will not be up to it, to say nothing of not being able to apply such honesty to oneself. But since placing a high value on friendship means that friends will be keenly sought, it is likely that such a life will be lived within quality circles of friends.

Plato also provides an account of one particular occasion when these tensions came to a head for Socrates in his relationship with an individual called Crito. Crito is an important friend of Socrates as far as history is concerned because he was present at Socrates' death. The occasion on which their friendship was put to the test was on the day of Socrates' execution, an encounter that Plato reconstructs in his dialogue called the *Crito*. The dialogue opens with Crito coming to Socrates in prison to tell him that the state galley is returning from Delos, a significant event because it marks the end of the religious festival during which Socrates, although condemned, could not be executed; with the return of the galley, his reprieve is over and it seems he must die. So Crito makes one last effort to persuade Socrates to allow his friends to pay off his jailers and secret him into exile. Socrates refuses. He wants to drink the poison and die rather than flee the city and live. Therein lies the quandary he faces in friendship. It is not that Socrates does not care about Crito. Quite the reverse; apart from the intimate and caring nature of their conversation, one reason why Socrates cannot escape is that to do so would implicate his friends who could then themselves face exile or injury. But more seriously as far as his beliefs about friendship are concerned, Socrates also knows that he must hold fast to what he holds to be true. Alongside the realisation of his wise ignorance, this includes the conviction that he should not be afraid of death. To run from the law would betray that conviction, though it is a burden he must ask his friend Crito to bear too. Moreover, to go against his philosophy would also be to go against his high ideal of friendship because his way of life as a philosopher and his search for true friendship – for another self – go hand in hand. Such is the price of honest friendship.

Other ways of honesty?

Now, there are a number of objections that can be raised against such high ideals of friendship. For example, is it not too unfeeling, harsh, and perhaps suspiciously drawn to a kind of flagellatory ambition? For some, perhaps the answer is yes. However, to see it only in this light would be to misunderstand its undoubtedly strong character. For one thing, not all friendships are asked to rise to this level of intensity, only those who would be friends of the deepest kind. And, it is important to remember the comments made by Nietzsche about bearing other people's faults because they bear your own: the harsher ideals that friendship might demand are offset by the uncompromisingly humane injunctions that friendliness requires too.

Alternatively, consider another comment Nietzsche makes: 'Fellow rejoicing, not fellow suffering, makes the friend.' Nietzsche's point is that given that it is natural to want to respond to a friend's distress in some way, it is better to respond positively. Create something, Nietzsche says, 'that the other can behold with pleasure: a beautiful, restful, self-enclosed garden perhaps, with high walls against storms and the dust of the doorway but also a hospital gate'. He connects this more joyful approach to previous times in history when the paucity of medical science meant that much suffering was unavoidable, in response to which people developed an ethic of rejoicing. They put their efforts into a culture of celebration rather than amelioration; happiness rather than pain. This idealisation of history can readily be questioned, of course: who wants to go to a party with toothache? But considering the dominance of reality TV, chat shows and agony columns, Nietzsche is surely right to point out that these theatres of cruelty have proliferated in the modern world for the very reason that the spectacle of others suffering and the opportunity it provides for us to show pity distracts us from, and relieves us of responsibility for, facing the truth of our own pain.

Another objection might be that even if such high ideals of friendship are not as harsh as they first seem because they appeal to a more genuine kind of compassion, are they still worth it? Are there not other ways to discover the truth of ourselves that do not require drawing others into the sometimes brutal truths of life? Or perhaps the effort that high friendship's penetrating honesty demands would be better placed elsewhere?

Some people have indeed concluded that truth is best sought not in friends but in substitutes for friends. Christina Rossetti, for one, wrote a poem about a tree, entitled with the ironic double entendre, 'A Dumb Friend'. One verse reads:

> So often have I watched it, till mine eyes
> Have filled with tears and I have ceased to see,
> That now it seems a very friend to me,
> In all my secrets wise.

More commonly, many might say that drowning the sorrow of their secrets in beer or wine is better and easier than bothering others; the alcohol seems like a good friend because it reflects their mood back to them.

More idiosyncratically, the Victorian art critic John Ruskin confessed that pictures were his only friends because they were the only things with which he could form honest attachments.

Or what of the case of a book as a friend? If 'the novelist lives in his work', as Joseph Conrad put it, then is not a book a friendship with a person, formed through its pages? A slightly different take on the idea of friendship with a book was expressed by Anne Frank. She famously called her diary Kitty, explaining that in the long hours of her hiding from the Nazis it was in a way a better friend than a person since 'paper is more patient than man'. In fact, a book appears to provide a good alternative of friendship with some-thing because what a book shares with some-one is the potential to impart objective self-understanding. For example, when we say we know a book well because we have returned to it several times, there is the implication that it resonates with our own experience, throws light upon it, and constantly reveals things to us about ourselves. Supreme examples would be religious books like the Bible or the Koran. Stanley Cavell, a contemporary American philosopher who has written on friendship, goes one step further and uses reading a book as itself an analogy for friendship, pointing out that in friendship one is able to 'read' the other and one allows oneself to be 'read'.

So, one can easily question whether a bottle of wine is really a good friend, unless you are an alcoholic. And the perpetual tree hugger is likely to be unbalanced. However, the case of the book is less easily resolved. Perhaps unexpectedly, Marcel Proust is someone who makes a strong case in its favour. He believed not just that friendship with people was unbearable unless individuals wear masks of good manners, a necessity that makes any real friendship impossible, but, more devastatingly still, he thought that people can never provide the opportunity for any real honesty anyway. In friendship, the greatest honesty that can be hoped for is a kindly acknowledgement that the request for friendship can never truly be given nor received. Books, however, overcome the limitations with which individuals find themselves encumbered when relating to one another. For example, Proust invites us to consider the fact that friendship depends on conversation. The trouble with conversation, he implied, is that it is flawed: people get sidetracked, exchange only commonplaces, cannot communicate considered positions, or respect each other's self-delusion without challenging it. Novels, though, as means of communication are everything that conversation is not. They are focused, innovative, considered and disinterested. Because of that, he concluded that there is a purity in reading to which friendship can never aspire; books have no false amiability. When you are finished with a book, you shelve it without offence, something that is impossible with a friend. Proust even went so far as to misquote Aristotle and say that a book is another self, though better than a friend since it is not susceptible to social habits, pressures or vices.

However, I think this is precisely why books will not, ultimately, do as friends. They may appear to be substitutes for friendship inasmuch as a spirit of honesty drives the desire to write and be read. But although books may be the product of another self, they are not 'an other self' as the adage implies in its deepest sense. For example, the control someone has over books may prevent false feeling but it indulges narcissism, the great enemy of self-honesty: a book is shelved with impunity when one does not like it because there is no obligation to respect it, like one must another person. Or, a book may open someone's eyes to difference but difference only fully confronts us and challenges us to change in an encounter with another human being. It is the irreducibility of these human elements that makes for the power-ful, if troubling, experience of deep friendship. And if conversation though drenched in goodwill is hardly ever entirely authentic, it is irre-placeable in conjuring up those rare moments of truth. Friendship of the honest sort may need the months and years of accommodation and propriety to produce it.

Solitude

A different kind of response to the ambiguities of honesty in friendship is to turn from it entirely. In fact, most scholars would probably say that this is what Nietzsche did in the last years of his life. In the books of his final period, the few comments he makes on friendship appear to advocate increasingly adversarial relationships that precipitate ever more courageous acts of overcoming, with the result that mere circles of friends come to be seen as a dangerous hindrance: 'every person is a prison, also a nook and a corner'. However, if we look at the sayings of the character Zarathustra whom he creates in *Thus Spoke Zarathustra*, a more subtle position emerges than merely a rejection of friends. It is one that reveals another perhaps surprising dimension to this theme of truthfulness in friendship.

Nietzsche's Zarathustra is a prophet named after the founder of the ancient Persian religion Zoroastrianism. Nietzsche thought the origi-nal Zarathustra remarkable because he had struggled in his times with how to speak truthfully, how to pierce the smoke and mirrors of verisimilitude, how 'to shoot well with arrows'. In other words, he personifies a spirit of honesty. He first appears in Nietzsche's book coming out of solitude in the mountains as a prophet. He then utters a series of soliloquies to whoever will listen, one of which is entitled 'Of the Friend'. What is striking about it is that Zarathustra speaks as a hermit who longs for friendship. This is clearly a paradoxical state of affairs. How can someone who wants to be alone also want a friend?

The answer is that the hermit does not really want to be alone for isolation's sake, but rather that he seeks a retreat in order to achieve the state of mind that is rid of the clutter of life and allows him to see clearly. The difficulty Zarathustra's hermit has got himself into is that his isolation has caused him to turn in on himself. Rather than finding clarity of mind, he finds himself having a conversation between the 'I and Me' in his mind that only leads to him 'sinking to the depths'.

This is where his desire for a friend comes in. The good friend is someone who can save the hermit from his downward spiral without destroying the tranquillity of mind that much human interaction brings and from which the hermit longs to be free. More colloquially, we might say that one can be alone with a friend. (There is another sense in which solitude can be good for friendship, namely, taking some time out to think about it! Reading or writing a book on friendship, activities that are mostly done in silence and alone, might provide a good case in point …). Nietzsche's advocacy of solitude, then, has two senses. First, it implies a solitary solidarity of friendship between those who are other selves to one another. If the friend knows the individual better than themselves, then honest friendship is an opportunity to be alone together with the truth about one another. Second, I think Nietzsche is also pointing to a role friendship can play not only at a personal level but also at a social one. Solitude, in this case, is an isolation of a different sort: it is a mental separation from a world which loathes rest and reflection and has what is more mundanely called the wrong work/life balance.

One thinks with a watch in one's hand, even as one eats one's midday meal while reading the latest news of the stock market; one lives as if one always 'might miss out on something'. 'Rather do anything than nothing': this principle, too, is merely a string to throttle all culture and good taste … Living in a constant chase after gain compels people to expend their spirit to the point of exhaustion in continual pretence and overreaching and anticipating others. Virtue has come to consist of doing something in less time than someone else. Hours in which honesty is permitted have become rare, and when they arrive one is tired and does not only want to 'let oneself go' but actually wishes to stretch out as long and wide and ungainly as one happens to be.

This way of life erodes the attention that is necessary for truthfulness. It is also strangely suspicious of joy for pleasure's sake – hence,

Nietzsche notes, that in the modern world when people are caught doing something pleasurable, like walking in the country, they excuse it as necessary for their health. This damages the capacity for deep friendship as much as anything else: 'Soon we may well reach the point where people can no longer give in to the desire for a *vita contemplativa* (that is, taking a walk with ideas and friends) without self-contempt and a bad conscience.' The concern is partly that friendship may come to be determined by utility, as it can be in the workplace. And partly that if honest friendship that acts as a counter-cultural force to the multiple, frequently inauthentic ways that people have of interacting with each other, then other virtues like character or spiritual insight will come to an end too.

Solitude with a friend is the antidote. Though, again, it is no easy option. The psyche is a complex entity and a cosy solitude can easily lead to a smug presumptuousness, on the one hand, or moroseness, on the other. Friends together may also go the way of the isolated hermit, turning in on each other:

> If we live together with another person too closely, what happens is similar to when we repeatedly handle a good engraving with our bare hands: one day all we have left is a piece of dirty paper. The soul of a human being too can finally become tattered by being handled too continually.

Truthfulness and honesty, not self-justification and self-indulgence are the test.

Ending friendship

The chapter began with a discussion of Nietzsche's break with Wagner. This has opened up a path through the play of dissimulation and difference, selfhood and solitude in friendship. However, it also points to the possibility that friendship may come to an end not just because people 'trivially' fall out, but because sometimes it may even be implicit in the dynamic of the friendship – as I have argued it was with Nietzsche and Wagner. What then on ending friendship?

To recap: within circles of friends, friendship comes under threat because people frequently find themselves skating on thin ice; cracks that open onto icy water are never far from the surface. Add to this risk the fact that friendship is a game that must usually be played out with many people at once. A new friend, for example, may give the game away because they have underestimated the subtlety of the rules by which the older friends are playing; the faux pas is easier to utter than the bon mots because it stems from ignorance not knowledge.

The closest of friends are not immune from the damage that can be caused by feelings of envy, distrust or betrayal too. In Shakespeare's *The Winter's Tale* two childhood friends, Leontes and Polixenes, fall out when Leontes suspects that Polixenes is having an affair with his wife, Hermione. 'Now my sworn friend and then mine enemy,' breaths Leontes: the friends who were yoked together in love are now yoked by that which 'did betray the Best'. It turns out that Leontes is mistaken. But before he realises that, his son has died as, apparently, have his wife and daughter. The perception of deception can be as damaging to friendship as actual deception itself, especially where it can exert the most damage – upon the intimacy of the closest friends.

As serious are the difficulties that arise when someone changes or moves, finds happiness or success. Prejudices that have been hidden since the foundation of the friendship can suddenly find themselves bursting at the seams – a double blow since it may well be that the friendship itself has opened up the new vista, as Nietzsche again laments:

> The best of them are lenient with us and wait patiently for us soon to find our way back to the 'right path' – they know, it seems, what the right path is! The others resort to mockery and act as though one had become temporarily insane, or they make spiteful allusions to the person they suppose to have misled us. The more malicious declare us to be vain fools and seek to blacken our motives, while the worst former friend of all sees in us his worst enemy and one thirsting for revenge for a protracted dependence – and is afraid of us.

However, in all these cases there are steps that can be taken before the end of the friendship is signed and sealed. Nietzsche's advice is a conciliatory approach: at the first sign of mockery or maliciousness offer the friend a year's amnesty during which they can reform their attitude. But what happens when the amnesty is not enough? Or, more generally, how should one treat a friendship when it breaks up whether by deliberate action or unavoidable accident?

Aristotle was alert to the pain and difficulty of ending friendships and devoted a whole chapter to it. He noted that the problem is particularly intense when someone thinks they are liked because of their character, for who they are in themselves, and it turns out that this was feigned and they are only liked because of their wallet or their wit. Worse still, when the usefulness ends or the pleasure the friends shared dries up, it is also easy for the one who has changed to feel duplicitous for having feigned the friendship to start with. 'Quarrels between friends occur more than anything when there is a difference between what they think the basis of the friendship is and what it actually is,' Aristotle wisely observes. In such cases, when very great offence is taken, there is little possibility of a good ending.

Another possibility Aristotle considers is whether friendships should be dissolved when one friend changes for the worst (to avoid the pretence that they are as likeable as they have always been)? This perhaps happens more than we would care to admit: principled character can be eroded by money or success; warm natures can become embittered by experience. With these changes the thing that was good about the friend, and that formed the basis of the friendship, goes too. Consequently, if the unchanged friend feels they can do little about it, the friendship will fade as faking it becomes too much. Sadly but honourably one might retain a memory of the intimacy that was shared in the past, Aristotle adds, and remember the former friend in a kindly way.

A third possibility arises from Nietzsche's concept of ladder-types. These friendships will feel under threat because although one or both friends have changed, and probably for the better, they will now be on different paths that may take them a long way apart. 'Star friendship' is Nietzsche's poetic way of describing this end to friendship:

> We were friends and have become estranged. But this was right, and we do not want to conceal and obscure it from ourselves as if we had reason to feel ashamed. We are two ships each of which has its goal and course ... and then the good ships rested so quietly in one harbour and one sunshine that it may have looked as if they had reached their goal and as if they had one goal. But then the almighty force of our tasks drove us apart again into different seas and sunny zone, and perhaps we shall never see each other again ... Let us then *believe* in our star friendship even if we should be compelled to be earth enemies.

The picture he draws is of a star in the heavens that memorialises the friendship, as it were, and which we might see if we look up. It can be appreciated there, for although it shines like the things that were shared, it no longer casts a shadow over the former friends' lives.

There is, then, such a thing as a good and a bad break in friendship. The good break is a consequence of the good thing that the friendship gave, the new path or insight, that then took the friends apart. The bad break is a consequence of negative change. Perhaps, in most breaks there is a mixture of both, like the split between Nietzsche and Wagner. Whatever; past friendships should lend themselves to future graciousness, for, even if it was a gift wrapped in thorns or conversely less of a gift than it first seemed, friendship brought a gift nonetheless. For that, it is remembered.

4
Unconditional Love

Because they love no one, they imagine that they love God.
Thomas Keneally

The fourth set of ambiguities associated with friendship to consider
next stem not only from factors inherent in the concept itself but also
as a result of the fallout from a particular, historical tragedy.

In 375 CE, Augustine of Hippo – Saint Augustine – returned from the
splendour of the Roman University at Carthage to his hometown
of Thagaste, an outpost of farmers now called Souk Ahras in Algeria.
A few years earlier, he had left as a pagan. He came back now a
Manichean. This illegal sect that believed in the radical separation of
good and evil was bound to appeal to the sometime student, now
young teacher. It brought him not only philosophical certainty but
also the fellowship of a cultivated group of friends. As he settled down
to teaching in Thagaste he quickly found a new set of Manichean
friends and established for himself a way of life that was a model of
classical friendship (something we know about from the record he
provides in his autobiographical *Confessions*).

All kinds of things rejoiced my soul in their company – to talk and
laugh, and to do each other kindnesses; to read pleasant books
together; to pass from lightest jesting to talk of the deepest things
and back again: to differ without rancour, as a man might differ
with himself, and when, most rarely, dissension arose, to find our
normal agreement all the sweeter for it; to teach each other and to
learn from each other; to be impatient for the return of the absent,
and to welcome them with joy on their homecoming; these, and
such-like things, proceeding from our hearts as we gave affection

and received it back, and shown by face, by voice, by the eyes, and by a thousand other pleasing ways, kindles a flame which fused our very souls together, and, of many, made us one.

Aristotle could not have described this happy life more accurately himself: 'Friendship is a kind of excellence and furthermore is very necessary for living.' Augustine even had a friend of the very best sort, someone who was another self, sweeter to him than all the other joys of life, he said.

Ancient philosophers were also never far from his mind. For example, the youthful prayer for which he is now well known – 'Lord give me chastity and continence: but not now' – is a troubled response to Cicero's description of the pleasures of the body as 'snares and the source of all ills': unlike many of his Manichean friends, Augustine had a concubine and did worry a little about the impact of this sensual indulgence upon the powers of his intellect. Though she was undoubtedly nice to have.

Then within a year of his return, the winding blow of calamity struck. His best friend developed a fever. He lost consciousness and, fearing for his life, was baptised by his Christian family. Augustine thought little of it at the time, believing that his friend would laugh at the ceremony when he revived. However, when his friend did rally, he turned on Augustine and warned him not to mock: he must accept his new faith or become his deadly enemy, he said. Augustine was stunned. He tried to comfort himself with the thought that his friend's belligerence was an after-effect of his illness, though it disturbed him enough to end his round the clock vigil at the sickbed. So when his friend's fever returned a few days later, Augustine was not there. Neither was he there when he died.

Augustine was now not just shocked, he was entirely overcome:

My own country became a torment and my own home a grotesque abode of misery. All that we had done together was now a grim ordeal. My eyes searched everywhere for him, but he was not there to be seen. I hated all the places we had known together, because he was not in them and they could no longer whisper to me 'Here he comes!' as they would have done had he been alive but absent for a while.

He was also tormented by the extent of the grief itself. It seemed to undo all his confidence. He told himself to wait for God's help but his soul refused to be comforted; he became afraid of death and was haunted by fantasies of other friends dying.

And then the horrible nub of it became clear in his mind. He realised that he loved the man he had lost more than he had ever loved God, and, worse still, that he loved himself even more than that. If he depended so utterly upon himself, a thing that could so easily pass away, was not his self-sufficiency a terrible conceit? 'What madness, to love a man as something more than human!' He lost faith in everything; we would say he had a breakdown. He could find no peace in people, books or poetry. He tired of himself. 'The god I worshipped was my own delusion, and if I tried to find in it a place to rest my burden, there was nothing there to uphold it.' Even the soil beneath his feet became synonymous with death and, much against the advice of his elders, he took his leave of Thagaste and left.

Back in Carthage, Manicheism provided some comfort and he took to writing a book on beauty as if by the effort he could restore his faith in the world. Time did heal the wounds of his immediate loss – but not those of the more profound crisis. The vertiginous (and very modern-sounding) fear of having to rely on himself was to haunt him for 11 more years, when he became a Christian.

This conversion transformed him. It saved him from himself, installing in place of his own divided will faith in Jesus Christ. He was overjoyed. However, the self-renunciation it entailed had serious implications for his belief in friendship. He started to look back on those early years with his friends and thought them vainglorious: 'In public we were cocksure, in private superstitious, and everywhere void and empty.' He came to the conclusion that they were all as deluded as each other and, because the things they loved were false, their friendship was false too. 'Ours was not the friendship which should be between true friends ... for though they cling together, no friends are true friends unless you, my God, bind them fast to one another through that love which is sown in our hearts by the Holy Ghost.' This explained why the death of his friend had been so overwhelming: it was not only that he had relied too much on his friend's love, but also that the friendship was really just a mirror of his love of himself. Thus, to lose a friend was to lose oneself. His Christian faith, in contrast, taught him something very different. When people love God and renounce their love of themselves, they can then love others with confidence. Their love is then primarily located in God and so unconditioned by the vagaries of life: 'They alone will never lose those who are dear to them, for they love them in one who is never lost, in God.'

Friendship is to be seen from the viewpoint of divine love – its ultimate end.

However, this 'friendship-in-God' ethos cast a shadow over human friendship. Although at one level it was aimed at recasting the compli-cated love of human friendship within the pure love of God, it meant, I think, that Augustine never quite recovered his faith in actual friend-ships again. For one thing, he came to see the death of his friend as an act of God's vengeance for his earlier misdirected love, though a vengeance tempered by mercy since it was also a crucial moment in ending the spell of his youthful, Manichean delusion. But, more pro-foundly, if the painful end of a friendship started him on his journey to his true home, eternity – 'which does not fall because we are away' – friendship itself was never going to seem quite the same again. Hence nearly forty years later, when he came to write *The City of God*, he cast friendship in a notably doubtful light. It can never be carefree, he said, because life is full of dangers. Friends will die or be parted from you, a tragedy and sadness whose likelihood increases the more friends one has. And worse, friends can betray you – in matters of state or affairs of the heart: indeed, there is a part of him that now rejoices when he hears of a friend's death for the very reason that that dreadful possibil-ity has ceased. As his modern biographer Peter Brown has put it:

> The man who had once thought that he could reach an ideal of per-fection fixed for him by the philosophical culture of his age, in the company of friends of recognizable quality, unambiguously marked out for the higher life by education and serious intentions, becomes filled with Romantic longings for states he would never achieve in this life, for friends he would never entirely know.

The loss of faith in friendship became 'the silent tragedy' of his later life.

From loss of faith to rejection

Augustine's story marks a pivotal moment in the philosophy of friend-ship. Many of the things that he wrestled with in friendship, such as its fragility and its relationship to love of self, were familiar to ancient philosophers including Aristotle and Plato. The fragility of friendship is arguably the defining feature of Plato's portrayal of friendship in the *Lysis* where Socrates confesses he does not have a true friend and does not even really know what friendship is. Aristotle examined the apparent contradiction of the second issue – that loving another depends on loving oneself – concluding that it is in fact unobjectionable because unless someone can befriend themselves they are hardly likely to able to form any deep friendships with others.

But where Augustine is different, and where he injects radically new Christian ideas, is in his response to these features of friendship; he comes to very different conclusions. First, friendship's fragility is not to be simply embraced but must be overwritten with the unconditionally reliable love of God. He suggests a kind of triangulation by which friends love each other through and in what his faith teaches him is a firm foundation. Second, he thought that friendship's inherent narcissism should be renounced. The individual who thinks that they can learn to love others by first learning to love themselves, as Aristotle suggested, is in fact inculcating a dangerous state of mind, a dependency upon the things of this world. Friendship in this mode is bound to fail in betrayals and partings, moments when the individual chooses or succumbs to something else. Whereas if this love of self is renounced, a new way of loving opens up that depends not on the weak will of the individuals concerned but on the constant will of God.

It is important to stress how alien both these moves would have seemed to Plato and Aristotle. The idea that self-renunciation is the key to the good life would have been antithetical to Aristotle's self-perfected man; he would have thought of self-renunciation as indistinguishable from self-abnegation. The right approach for him was to find a middle path between that extreme and its opposite, self-conceit. With the right balance an individual can then cultivate a good kind of selfishness – wanting to become the best kind of person they can in ways that are in turn of benefit to others.

When it comes to Augustine's second move, that individuals should rely on the love of God, the ancients would have been equally uncomprehending. They tended to think that although people rightly worship gods and honour them for the qualities they possess, to associate friendship with the divine was a mistake. Aristotle argued that one would no more locate one's friendship in a god than one would in a king: both are superior and friendship is nothing if the friends are not in the same boat.

So the Augustinian intervention in ideas about friendship has a correspondingly significant effect on the way friendship is valued. The Christian response was not to seek philosophical resolutions to the ambivalences inherent in the concept, as the ancients had, but was to question the very virtuousness of friendship itself. Alternatively, if self-betterment is replaced by self-renunciation, as Augustine argues, then friendship is inevitably downgraded in the hierarchy of values. Further, if the chief characteristics of friendship, that it is particular and in a certain sense selfish, are subsumed within the defining characteristic of Christian love, that is universal and selfless, it is easy to dismiss friendship outright.

That may seem a bit extreme but it is a logical outcome of Augustine's anxieties about friendship and is a position that has been advocated by Christians. Perhaps the clearest case in point is found in the writings of the theologian Søren Kierkegaard. This nineteenth-century Dane (whose surname means graveyard) once said that he wrote to make life more difficult for people. He certainly throws down the gauntlet for any Christian writer on friendship, crystallising the essence of the Augustinian problem with friendship to such a degree that it becomes an outright rejection of friendship as such. In his *Works of Love*, he begins by asking what friendship is in its purest form. The answer, he says, is that it is a passion whose ideal is as exclusive as erotic love; whilst friendliness may be offered to many, friendship's finest image of itself is a love that makes two, and only two, one. From this preference that friends show one another all the other manifestations of its selfishness follow. Choosing you, the friend says, is *my* choice (Kierkegaard does not buy the Aristotelian reading of the friend as 'an other self'. For him, the relationship is not I–Other, it is I–other–I). Kierkegaard also points out that friendship is as prone to jealousy as erotic love and similarly cannot bear to have its love rejected (because to have one's affection returned is to confront one's narcissism with the possibility that one is not lovely). Alternatively, he notes that friendship, like erotic love, arises spontaneously from an individual's affection – it 'self-ignites' – and is not a voluntarily act of will; people arbitrarily 'fall in friendship' as much as they randomly fall in love. And then friendship gets caught up in all kinds of little acts of pride in the way that people congratulate themselves on their friends; they admire themselves for being so clever as to admire their admirable friend, and so on.

Given this negative assessment of friendship, the question arises as to the correct way for Christians to love one another as, after all, the law requires. The answer, Kierkegaard says, is the diametric opposite of friendship, namely, to love your *neighbour*. Neighbour-love is wholly different from friendship because it is unconditional and selfless: 'Christian love teaches love of all men, unconditionally all', and any exception to this unconditionality is a compromise. This means that there is no way, according to Kierkegaard, to integrate a notion of friendship into neighbour-love. It may be thought that loving one's neighbour begins with loving one's friends. Wrong, says Kierkegaard, because to love one's friend is to practise selfishness not selflessness. Or some Christians might claim that Christian love is like classical love but for the fact that it is stronger, loving unto death. Wrong, says Kierkegaard; there are endless examples of this so-called perfection of love in classical culture.

Another question that comes to mind is who is your neighbour if they are not your friends? Kierkegaard comes up with an disarmingly simple answer. The first person you meet as you go out of your door. The next human. In fact, and not without some wit, Kierkegaard argues that neighbour-love is a blessed release from the burden of having to find someone to befriend. It does not require you to admire your neighbour. Neither does loving your neighbour depend in any way on being able to love yourself. Rather it depends on renouncing yourself. (Neither should neighbour-love be thought of as a higher form of friendship. Neighbour-love abhors the idea that individuals can be united in a single self on the basis that they are the same, or indeed different. They love each other simply because they are equal before God who loves all equally and unconditionally. There is no continuity between the two; unconditionality cannot be reconciled to particularity nor selflessness to selfishness.)

If someone protests that this does not sound like love at all since it is passionless, Kierkegaard says they are mistaken too. The selfish passion of friendship gives way to the selfless passion to obey God, to fulfil the obligation of eternal love. 'Christian love is self-renunciation's love and therefore trusts in this *shall*.' And finally if someone else thinks that such a position is extreme to the point of ridiculousness and only causes offence, Kierkegaard retorts that what might be a stumbling block to some is the heart of the blessedness of Christianity to others. If you want to overcome the tragic disappointments of friendship then make that leap of faith! True to his name, Mr Kierkegaard does his best to bury friendship.

But what does one man's rant, let alone another man's loss of faith 1500 years ago, matter to us in the so-called secular world today? It matters because Kierkegaard's stance is not the only product of the long shadow that Augustine's tragedy has cast. Much secular thought is similarly wary of friendship too – and sometimes as out-rightly antagonistic. Indeed, far from dissipating over the intervening years, the shadow could be argued to have intensified because when cut loose of the Christianity that gave birth to it (and which at least values love), it takes on a life of its own. This is a big claim but it is one that can be seen to hold water if we cut to another seminal figure in the story, Immanuel Kant.

Christian secularism

Beyond his enormous influence, not least of the reasons for looking at what Kant has to say about friendship is that he is one of the rare philosophers since the Enlightenment to address the subject at all. If you turn to Descartes, Hobbes, Spinoza, Hume, Rousseau, Bentham, Mill, Hegel or Marx you will simply not find enough to go on. Kant though included sections on friendship in one of his books, *Metaphysics of Morals*, and he also gave a lecture on friendship as part of the course he taught at the University of Königsberg from 1775 to 1780. It provides a neat summary of secular modernity's equivocal attitude towards friendship.

The lecture begins by addressing what he sees as the familiar crux of the problem. Human beings are driven by two imperatives; their self-love and their love of others. Kant has a problem with self-love that refines the Christian concern. It worries him because although its selfish acts may not break any moral laws (i.e. they can be of benefit to others), neither can they be said to have any moral merit of their own (because they are motivated by selfishness): selfless acts, however, explicitly seek to promote the happiness of others and can rightly be thought virtuous.

This is bad news for the morality of humanity's behaviour because people act mostly out of their own self-interest, that is, amorally. Kant's neat way around this bleak prospect is his famous categorical imperative. He accepts that people will act in their self-interest but points out that it is also in someone's self-interest to have others acting in their interest too. So in order that everyone's interests are taken care of, each person must do to others as they would have them do unto themselves. Or, to put it another way: act only in such ways as would conform to a universal law – that is, make no exceptions for yourself, else others will do the same, and your own self-interest will be threatened.

The problem for friendship is how it can act morally within this frame. For example, Kant continues, if someone tries to act for the happiness of their friend, it is highly likely that they will have to subordinate their own happiness, a situation which would not seem to make for very happy friendships. Conversely, if they decide to prioritise their selfish desires and look after their own happiness first and foremost, then it is very likely that they will ride roughshod over the happiness of others, and that too seems counterproductive.

Maybe there is a way out of this conundrum, Kant wonders. Perhaps someone can look after the happiness of their friend without worrying about their own happiness, because their friend will be doing exactly the same for them? In other words, friendship is presented as a pact in which individuals put their selfish motives to one side because they know that their interests will be foremost in the mind of their friend, and vice versa. This, Kant says, is the ideal in friendship; a self-love that is 'superseded by a generous reciprocity of love'.

Now, this is again a neat logical trick. But it does not really absolve friendship of its selfishness; it just puts it at one step removed. Kant's reinterpretation of the Aristotelian idea of a friend as another self reveals the underlying selfish calculation in this reading of friendship and the associated moral duplicity. He says that the friend is another self not in the sense that they are similar or share goals, but in the sense that they love the other as if it were themselves. So even on his best account, Kant cannot shake off the suspicion that friendship is selfish. It might lead someone to act for another but only, if paradoxically, for wholly selfish reasons.

The dubious moral worth of friendship is compounded by the fact that this so-called generous reciprocity of love only takes place in the ideal case. In practice, Kant believes, no one can look after their own happiness better than they themselves and should someone surrender their happiness entirely to another in the hope of complete reciprocity, the friendship would inevitably fail. This is why in life people never actually call on their friends in the way that they call on themselves; rather than make such demands on others they will usually revert to doing things for themselves. Similarly, people may have one or two friends with whom they feel they can be completely open, but in reality they always hold things back in order not to disturb the illusion of friendship – another manifestation of amicable dissimulation. (This is also why to demand proof of friendship is the best way of ending it, Kant reflects, though he adds that the disposition of goodwill encouraged by a permanent attitude of never quite realised friendship is delightful in its own way.)

Friendship's suspect nature is also revealed in other ways. For example, people may form circles of friends on the basis that they share the same beliefs, interests or identity. But again these gestures are morally suspect because they tend to harden the heart against those outside the charmed circle.

Kant hints that the effort to make oneself deserving of friendship may be of some moral worth as a result of a strange twist of the obligations imposed by the categorical imperative: it is a person's duty to respect other people's friends because that is what they hope for in return, lest their own illusions about friendship are shattered. 'Friendship develops the minor virtues of life,' he concludes, damning it with faint praise. All in all, the morally ambiguous status of friendship is really left unchallenged.

In ethical no-man's-land

So much for Kant. But to see why his attitude towards friendship matters within secular ethics as a whole, think of the following simple case. Suppose someone lives in a boarding house with a shared bathroom and fellow tenants whom they do not know. The strangers have good reason to leave the bathroom clean and tidy after washing because only then can they hope with impunity that others in the house will do so as well. In other words, there is good reason for these strangers to be equally bound by an unwritten law of 'bathroom cleanliness'.

Now consider someone else who lives in a shared house with friends. Their relationship to their cohabitants is entirely different. They do not think of them as strangers but as unique individuals whom they know. This may cause them to act selflessly sometimes – when, for example, they clean the bathroom after their inveterately messy friend. But it may also cause them to act selfishly if, for example, that same friend happens to leave the bathroom dirty one too many times and they get annoyed.

The point is that in the first case there is a universalisable law governing bathroom cleaning, whereas in the latter case there is not. The reason? Friendship; it makes an individual behave inconsistently.

Clearly this is a somewhat comical case. But it makes the general point: modern ethics finds it hard to cope with friendship because if everyone acted solely as they do with friends, there could be no universalisable moral laws. (For similar reasons, friendship sits uneasily alongside moral theories that work on the basis that it is best to act so as to maximise people's welfare. This means that a good action is one that achieves the greatest happiness. But friendship can play little part in this moral scheme because, as friends, friends are interested predominantly in each other, not in the general happiness of all.)

The net result is that friendship occupies a moral no-man's-land today. Because it is at best wrestling with selfishness, and at worst positively encouraging it, it gets pushed to the margins of moral behaviour. In fact, Kant was so uneasy about the place of friendship in his moral universe that he speculated upon a time when friendship will cease. He wonders if human society will advance to such a stage of luxury that people will stop having needs and so similarly stop having need of friends. This will be a time in which people have a broader set of goals than the mere satisfaction of needs; a kind of heaven on earth that insofar as it is heavenly will have transcended the need for friendship. He summarises: 'Friendship is not of heaven but of the earth; the complete moral perfection of heaven must be universal; but friendship is not universal.'

All in all, what Kant achieves is a reinvention of the reactionary attitude to friendship that originates in Augustinian Christianity, reinvigorated for the modern, secular world. For a full-blown belief in heaven he substitutes an ideal of perfection; for sinfulness, selfishness; for unconditional love, universal obligation. This new 'religious' language of universal duty and categorical imperatives simply does not know what to do with friendship, and tends to think that it is suspect and better done away with. 'It is no wonder that friendship has been relegated to private life and thereby weakened in comparison to what it once was,' reflects the contemporary moral philosopher Alasdair MacIntyre. So, contemporary ethical discourses adopt an attitude towards friendship that is as detrimental to it as any Christian one. For example, why is it that if someone promotes a friend to work alongside them, it is unequivocally branded as nepotism with no thought given to whether they are up to the job or not? More generally, why is it that modern society has no public means of recognising friends, a fact that is in stark contrast to the family which is celebrated as the very basis of community? This is a complex issue to which we shall return, but is it not in part because friendship is treated as a selfish concern: unlike the family which gives something to society, friends are thought to be mostly interested in themselves, so society is hesitant in supporting it?

If the suspicion of anything that even smacks of selfishness is still detrimental to friendship, then the priority given to unconditionality in modernity marginalizes it even more. Consider the impact on friendship of the value assigned to egalitarianism – the idea that everyone should be treated the same. It lies at the heart of modern democracy; in theory at least, everyone has equality before the law and the right to one, and only one, vote. The power of the rhetoric of human rights rests on its claim to be unconditional too: either rights are universal or they are nothing at all. 'This equality absolutely every man has, and he has it absolutely' (that quote is not from the convention on human rights but from Kierkegaard on neighbour-love but it significantly works equally well in both places). Of course, this kind of unconditionality can be hugely valuable and underpins many great goods. However, the trouble for friendship is that it is not unconditional, but conditional – one would do something for a friend and not others. Thus, within this moral frame, friendship is routinely treated as if it were questionable. The contrast with the family again provides a ready case in point. It is not just that friendship is not recognised in society, whereas family is, but the particularity of friendship can often be regarded as a threat to the unconditional love that is supposed to reign within the family too. For example, why do individuals somehow feel they should renegotiate a long-term friendship just because their friend gets marriage? Or, to put it another way: is there not a steely strand in the ethic of modern marriage which repels anything that compromises the unconditional commitment of husband and wife; 'forsaking all others', the service says? Particular friendship can count as infidelity quite as much as a fling or affair.

This is a deeply unsatisfactory state of affairs. For all Kant may wish it, and ethical discourse may ignore it, friendship will not cease! Aristotle's intuition is right: it may be a bit selfish, and it is certainly particular, but it is also undoubtedly necessary for a happy life. Moreover, if friendship is rising back up the agenda of people's personal commitments, as marriage reshapes and other institutions of belonging become less reliable, then an ethical discourse that takes friendship seriously is needed, not least to provide some suggestions for people who want to make the most of it. Friendship will always be full of ambiguities; I hope this book has by now established that. But that does not mean it is not possible to think through them and welcome friendship as a key, if complicated, facet of life.

It turns out that a resurrection of friendship has been attempted before. A number of more friendship-friendly theologians have sought to find a place for friendship that reconciles it to the principles that would otherwise damn it. One attempt stands out; that of Thomas Aquinas. He is first among equals with Augustine as a doctor of the Church and has also been called one of the greatest interpreters of Aristotle, an accolade that might give us hope that he thought highly of friendship. He is also important because his thought led to a distinction that is critical if modern, secular attitudes towards friendship are to be revivified – the distinction between egoistic and altruistic love. (He did not use these terms himself, as I shall in discussing him, but the origins of egoism and altruism are found in the distinctions he draws and are convenient in unpacking what he says.) So now let us take a step from modern secularism back to medieval Christianity, and see what resources for us lie there.

Reaffirming friendship

Thomas – he is known as Thomas and his philosophy as Thomism because Aquinas is a place not a name – was born in 1225 at a seminal moment in the history of Western ideas. For most of the Middle Ages, Roman philosophy including the works of Cicero and Seneca had formed the staple diet of an education in Latin, and Greek philosophy was virtually unknown. Then during the twelfth century a handful of Aristotelian texts in Latin translation began to find their way into the universities of Europe and by the end of the thirteenth century, Thomas's century, virtually all Aristotle's surviving works were well known. A major figure in this undertaking was a Dominican colleague of Thomas, William of Moerbeke, who tackled not only Aristotle's vast corpus but also ancient commentaries on him too, 'by dint of great toil and much mental tedium', he writes in one place. An important translation of the *Nicomachean Ethics* containing Aristotle's reflections on friendship was completed in 1247 by an English philosopher who went by the name of Grosseteste. And by the time Thomas became a professor of theology in Paris at the age of 30, Aristotle was so dominant that he was commonly known simply as 'the Philosopher'.

Aristotle's leading interpreter at the time was the Muslim philosopher Ibn Rushd usually called Averroes (and correspondingly called 'the Commentator'). It was the Commentator who determined Thomas's life's work: the Christianisation of Aristotle.

Averroes had made two observations that unless challenged were fatal to Aristotle's reception in the Church. First, he said that the Philosopher thought the world was eternal and, second, that he thought individual souls were mortal. Christianity teaches precisely the opposite on both counts (heaven is eternal not the world, and souls are immortal and go to heaven) and as a consequence Aristotle aroused great suspicion in ecclesiastical circles, even provoking a series of papal bulls that on occasion went so far as to ban him from the lecture halls of Paris and Oxford. Thomas's great achievement was to find an accommodation between these incendiary doctrines and the tenets of Christianity, an accommodation that secured Aristotle's fundamental place in Western thought to this day.

Thomas's philosophy of friendship is ingenious too. It is found in his *Summa Theologiae* whose second part is modelled on the *Nicomachean Ethics* (a choice which makes the Christian problem with the love called friendship unavoidable). As we have seen, Aristotle caused difficulties because he focused on the idea that friendship is particular and based on self-love. Thomas changes the focus of the debate by arguing two things. First, although friendship can be for oneself or for another, that does not mean that it is not of benefit to both parties *in both cases*. For example, friendship based on utility or pleasure is primarily for oneself but can also contain elements that the friend benefits from too. This kind of friendship, says Thomas, may not be especially virtuous but neither is it necessarily evil; in essence it is no better or worse than the desire to eat or to own. And friendship that is explicitly for another is a love that although primarily for the other person and their sake also benefits the individual giving the friendship. It is a friendship that is disinterested in what can be gained from the relationship but which gains nonetheless.

Thomas's second point follows on from this. Given that friendship always benefits both parties, if to varying degrees, the real offence to God's love is to be found in the extent to which the friendship on offer is possessive or not. Love always wants. (Indeed, Thomas thought that everything humans do is done out of some kind of love, some kind of want.) The thing that determines whether love is godly is the extent to which it is focused on the good of the other person or the good of the individual: love that tends to the former is what we now call altruistic love, love that is for the other but benefits both; love that tends to the latter is what we now call egoistic love, love that is for oneself but benefits the other if only as a by-product.

Friendship reveals itself as either altruistic or egoistic in several ways. For example, an altruistic friendship is one in which if something happens to one friend or something is said against them, the other person in the relationship feels it as if they were themselves being hurt or maligned; they will oppose anything that might harm their friend as if it were harming themselves. In an egoistic friendship, however, someone will only go out on a limb when they are directly threatened themselves.

A related test concerns how someone relates to the friends of their friend. When characterised by altruism, that person will be friendly to them for the sake of their friend, even if their friendliness is not readily returned. Conversely, the egoistic individual will make little effort with the friend of a friend, and in all likelihood unpleasantness with this third party will cause the original friendship to break down too.

Another key indicator is provided because such is the extent of the mutual feeling of altruistic friendship, or 'indwelling' as Thomas calls it, that to onlookers this kind of friendship looks more like a habit than a passion. The friends come to routinely act for each other. When it comes to relating to others, generosity and kind-heartedness become similarly overarching principles in their lives, a quality of relating that is reflected in everything they do. Those who only befriend in egoistic ways, in contrast, will not internalise such love to anything like this degree.

Thomas also explains that altruistic friendship forms between people who are alike or equal in what they have or are, whereas egoistic friendship tends to dominate when one person has something that the other ardently desires. Think, for example, of a friendship between someone who is famous and someone else who is not. Fame is so alluring that it is hard for the friends of the famous not to want at least some of the glory. This means that they are likely to form egoistic friends and friendship will only flourish in the altruistic sense if the unknown person is indifferent to the fame. In fact, the best opportunities for altruistic friendship arise when it is based upon something that is good in itself – Thomas would cite Christian virtues like love, joy, peace or patience. To put it another way, these are qualities that are inherently altruistic and so tend to make a friendship based upon them more altruistic and less egoistic too.

This fluidity, this sense that even egoistic friendships contain elements of goodness, means that there is the possibility that even the most selfish friendships need not be thought irredeemably tainted (as long as the relationship clings onto being worthy of the name to some degree). Traces of altruism can still flourish, like light that drives away darkness. Consider an individual who forms a friendship with another who seems at peace with themselves for the reason that they long for peace too. That might be thought to make it egoistic. But since longing for peace is the first step to gaining it, and since peace is a virtue that tends to be generous to others, the individuals who are otherwise unequal in their peacefulness, as it were, can find common ground between them that makes for an increasing altruistic friendship.

Thomas can similarly recognise that friendship has mixed motives and is based upon loving the complex particularities of another individual who also has egoistic and altruistic intentions. It is the details of anyone's life that counts for a friendship to form, be it their virtues, interests or needs, things that will always be expressed altruistically and egoistically. (This is also a reflection of the commonsensical assumption that one good person will not automatically be friends with another solely because they are both good.) Further, he sees that it is only natural that an individual will be closer to some people than they are to others, and that a particular intimacy does not necessarily negate more distant relationships. Indeed, he goes a step further again and explicitly points out that it is only natural for someone to love *themselves* more than their neighbour, at least in their best parts, since they are a unity and so 'closer to themselves' than anyone else. This introverted love of oneself can still have an altruistic dimension though. If, for example, I followed a wholly selfless commandment to love my neighbour, I might take that to include an act like pushing them off a cliff if they sincerely wanted it. However, if I have love of myself too that would prevent the action inasmuch as I would be deterred by having to live with the consequences – a selfish considera- tion that would lead to someone else's good.

The general point for Thomas is that people may love others to greater or lesser degrees but it is not quantity but quality that counts (loving less is still loving). In fact, because friendship can be an over- arching principle in someone's life, a close friendship is likely to make that person love others more, even when they barely know them.

Now, Thomas was writing on friendship nearly six hundred years before Kierkegaard and in most respects they are theologically even further apart. However, he does provide a remarkably full response to Kierkegaard's hatchet job. Where Kierkegaard says that friendship is selfish, Thomas says don't overlook the altruistic dimension to friend- ship that is a selfless love for another. Where Kierkegaard says that the union friends seek is inherently exclusive, Thomas says don't forget that the closer altruistic friends become the more they will seek to act lovingly to their friend's friends even when they receive animosity in return. Where Kierkegaard says that love should be unconditional and friendship is always particular, Thomas says it is wrong to think that particular friendship cannot lead to a more universal love because altruistic friendship nurtures natural affection, not undermines it. Where Kierkegaard says that friendship is just like erotic love in its desire solely to possess, Thomas says it is in fact different precisely at that point. Where Kierkegaard says the Christian should act uncondi- tionally and without distinction to all, Thomas points out the differ- ence between benevolence, which is the intention to do good, and beneficence, which is the act of doing good and bound to be limited, even in a saint. Finally, where Kierkegaard says the Christian should act out of obligation, a leap of faith in response to God's commandment that 'you shall love your neighbour', Thomas says the Christian acts in response to God's love which is itself a supreme kind of altruistic friendship. In fact, Thomas notes that whereas in the New Testament the commandment refers to neighbour, in the Old Testament the Levitical code says you shall love your *friend* as yourself. (In fairness to Kierkegaard, this is a contentious point. The old Greek and Latin bibles that Thomas knew did use a word for friend, as did the fourteenth-century vernacular translation by Wycliffe. However, by the Tyndale and King James versions, the word friend had been replaced by neighbour, though not least because of the problems that loving friends evokes.) In summary, what Thomas would point out to Kierkegaard is that he has not taken the subtleties of the movement between altruistic and egoistic love seriously enough. He might also gently say to Augustine that he too saw his friendship mostly in terms of its egoistic elements, perhaps something that is inevitable following the shock of his friend's death when he was left with only himself to think of.

Thomas, then, goes a long way to rehabilitate friendship in the Christian era. He even finds a partial reconciliation between the Christian idea of friendship with God and the classical view that such a thing is impossible. If God is taken as a principle of love, then locating friendship in God can be reinterpreted as a process by which the friends and their friendship is transformed by that divine principle. On that reading, this is not so different from Aristotle's idea that the best kind of friendships are those in which the friends' lives are transformed by the good life.

However, for inhabitants of the modern world, Thomas only takes us half way. He provides the first step that links the classical world of Aristotle with the Christian world of the Middle Ages. We must now try to make another step to span the gulf which exists between the Middle Ages and modernity, and ask whether Thomas provides the kind of resources that can challenge the negative attitudes towards friendship found in secular ethics.

Against atomism and absolutes

To do this, take a second look at the moves Thomas makes. His rehabilitation of friendship was achieved by questioning the grounds on which it was thought morally dubious; he unpicks the knot of selfish particularity tied round it. For example, he pointed out that because people love those to whom they are close, it is only natural for them to love themselves to whom they are closest. But that does not mean they love others less. Look at the mutual indwelling of friendship and the altruistic zeal that one friend can feel for another.

At a deeper level, what this argument points out to the modern mind is that individuals are inherently connected to one another. Thomas is able to say that selfless acts can emerge from self-love, and that altruism and egoism are not polar opposites, because his idea of individuality is blurred at the edges. This contrasts with the atomistic, autonomous Kantian individual who is more or less bound to go about the world worrying over their selfish desires to excess. Modern ethics likewise tends to see people as billiard balls, smashing into one another as each tries to maintain its course. Thus, reconciling one individual's happiness to another's is treated as a problem – as is friendship.

But perhaps human beings are more like creatures of clay who are formed and moulded by mutual contact and even, on occasion, become attached. (In fact, a number of wider concerns are encouraging a notion of connectedness in contemporary moral debates, from global environmental calamity to the problems of social alienation.) In that case, the choice between one person's happiness and another's does not seem so stark: my happiness is your happiness, the friend says; if I care for you, I care for myself, and vice versa. Alternatively, such connectedness can be thought of in relation to the question of utility and friendship. If someone feels blatantly used, as they too often do in the workplace, then the selfish aspect dominates and stymies friendship. If, in contrast, someone relies on a friend, they may still be using them to a degree but with an appreciative need that is also an opportunity to give. In the generosity of that kind of non-calculating exchange – when people are as glad to give as receive – the individuals draw closer and the friendship can flourish.

The second aspect of Thomas's move was to develop the inclusive character of divine love. In effect, he does not allow the idea that the unconditional is best to become the enemy of the particular which is good. For example, he argued that the love of someone in particular can be seen as a gift through which someone learns of wider concepts of love. In fact, he went so far as to conclude that God represents friendship. (This is another thing he might gently say to Augustine: your experience of the death of your friend was, in a sense, an experience of a loss of God. That is why it was so shocking, not because you didn't love God but for the very opposite reason. You loved God in your friend and despaired when he was gone.)

With this aspect of his argument, the challenge is to translate his scholastic and theistic arguments into a modern and non-theistic frame. This is harder to do because there are certain beliefs which are key to his reaffirmation of friendship and simply incommensurate with modern times. For example, he makes claims that are impossible for an atheist to embrace, such as the idea that God is friendship. Even for many theists such a notion may seem strange.

However, Thomas also refers to God as a 'principle of love', an ethical as opposed to theological notion, that perhaps helps us find a way around the problem. It is even possible to go a step further and substitute the idea of God with that of good, agreeing with Iris Murdoch: 'Good is the magnetic centre towards which love naturally moves.' If this is believable, then it is possible to follow Thomas's argument in this way. His dependence upon a certain idea of God that transforms friendship, rather than reducing it to merely human love, becomes a principle of love that can operate as a regulative function in all sorts of morally ambiguous situations that the rule of unconditionality cannot countenance. This principle (not ideal) of good is less vertical, more horizontal; less universal, more applicable; less absolute, more conditioned. To be fair to Kant he sees the ideal of friendship a bit like this too: 'this standard is employed as a measure of lesser qualities'. The trouble is that his is a measure that invariably finds actual friendship wanting. An alternative ethic of good friendship would substitute such unforgiving abstractions with more humane sentiments; the governing standard should be principled direction not tyrannical rule.

Another way to translate the theological aspects of Thomas's thought is to understand that his ethics are in a holistic frame. For him, it was humanity's journey to God that provided the frame. For us, it can be a conception of the ethical life that aims at what is good. Within philosophy, the school of thought that promotes this way of thinking is often called virtue ethics. The idea is that instead of thinking of moral philosophy as a series of problems that need to be solved by sets of rules, one thinks of moral philosophy as nurturing a way of life organised around certain virtues and encouraging them to flourish. This is, in fact, very much in the Aristotelian way of things. His *Nicomachean Ethics* includes friendship amongst a list of virtues that the individual should foster in order to have a happy life. Such an approach does not mean that all the ambiguities associated with friendship are automatically resolved. Indeed, most of Aristotle's discussion of friendship is about them. But because friendship is placed high on the list of things that are necessary for a happy life right at the outset of his moral philosophy, it does prevent it being marginalised in favour of more easily handled, though less humanly valuable, qualities (like, I would argue, neighbour-love).

Trust in friendship

Clearly, there is a lot more that could be said about this – indeed that *needs* to be said about it, given the compromised status of friendship in modern, secular ethics. However, by way of concluding this chapter, I want to draw attention to another facet of Thomas's rehabilitation of friendship that is, I think, at least as important. For apart from engaging with the ethics of friendship on rational grounds, he also seeks to address the fundamental difficulty raised by Augustine's tragic experience of it. He lost faith in friendship. Thomas seeks to restore it. A restoration of trust in friendship is also vital today.

Briefly consider Thomas's approach one more time. In challenging the assumption that friendship is purely selfish, he does not only untangle the issue intellectually but also tries to restore some faith in the complexities of human motivation by pointing out that selfish desires can include selfless intentions. Alternatively, one of the things he achieves in calling God a friend is to unsettle the assumption that God's love is distant and transcendent. This simultaneously questions the related ethical assumption that unconditional universality is preferable to conditional particularity. (In a post-Kantian idiom, an equivalent would be to point out that it is a mistake to think that all morally important imperatives are categorical. Rather it is worth trusting situations, like those in which friendship is operating, because unequivocally good behaviour may arise from equivocal and mixed motives.)

In other words, contemporary ethics needs to re-incorporate a dimension of trust into its account of friendship, not in the sense of acknowledging that friends trust each other but in the sense that moral philosophy itself needs to trust friendship as a way of life and guide to action. It is at this level that friendship has been most deeply damaged. Secularism's distrust of friendship has stymied the ethical climate within which it might thrive as successfully as any Christian patriarch's declaration that it is sinful and offends God. The contemporary reliance on the ethics of rights and egalitarianism is proof enough: friendship is thought to offend these absolute ideals.

Trust is about making a judgement, as Onora O'Neill has pointed out: will I place or refuse to place my trust in someone or something? If the place of friendship is to be restored, this is the decision that moral philosophy needs to make, namely, to trust friendship again. It needs to recognise that its motivations may be complex but they are not psychopathic; its affection may focus on just a few individuals but it need not be perniciously exclusive. What is more, if someone who says they love humankind pays little attention to friendship, it is right to think something is out of balance. Might not secular humanism be guilty of that?

5
Civic Friendship

There is little of friendship in tyrannies but more in democracies.

Aristotle

The first four chapters of this book have examined the pressures that utility, sexuality, dissimulation and post-Christian ethics exert on friendship. In each case, friendship finds itself confronting a threat and seeking out an opportunity. With utility, the threat to friendship comes from the suspicion of being used. In a utilitarian culture, such as obtains in the workplace, this is compounded by the diminishment of excellence for excellence's sake. People are valued for outcomes, they tend to be thought of as means to ends, and when treated as such become, in Adam Smith's word, unlovely. Alternatively, when people do things together, share a common project or strive for goals a great opportunity exists for friendship. The key is to get to know those concerned for whom they are so that when the work or utility disappears the friendship does not.

With sexuality, the competition between the demands of erotic love and the hopes of friendship might trouble relationships of all shades of affection and, if it does, eros often seems to hold sway. But if a passionate as opposed to a merely sexual element in the relationship gains the upper hand, and the desire to get to know the other person in mind and spirit grows, then the possessive love of lovers can give way to the wider aspirations of friends.

With the third issue of dissimulation, the nub is that often friendship rests on feigning. Most friends, consciously or not, know that there are no-go areas in the relationship and they don't go there for the sake of the friendship; you put up with my disagreeable foibles, attitudes or weaknesses and I will put up with yours. In fact friends generally rub along rather well and trouble only arises when goodwill and accommodation are perceived as dubiety and duplicity. But friendship can also on occasion rise above the mundane – and in rather wonderful ways. A moment of frankness and receptive humility comes about and the friend who is another self can speak words of truth to one, words that might even transform a life.

Finally, there are the ambiguities of the Christian legacy on friendship. In the extreme case, Christianity fosters a tyranny of unconditional love, manifest in so-called secular times as the requirement that ethics be universally applicable: both find the particular love of friendship seriously wanting. Linked to this is the suspicion that friendship is essentially selfish and therefore morally dodgy. Friendship suffers first at the level of ethical discourse, an attitude towards it that, second, percolates down so that it comes to be seen as, say, divisive in relation to family and corrupting in the workplace or politics.

Each of these sets of ambiguity – the perils to friendship, and the related promise – are set in a broader context, namely, contemporary society. This is self-evidently true in the case of the Christian inheritance and its influence upon modern ethics. When utility undermines friendship it does so in part because the development of deeper friendships is stunted in a culture that in practice values productivity over praiseworthiness. With sexuality, eros tends to hold sway because we live in a romanticised, sexualised society. Even the art of speaking truthfully in friendship has a social dimension because it requires time: a culture that tends to think that friends can be made in an instant, and are limited in quantity only by the number of people you meet, tips the balance between dissimulation and honesty in favour of the former. Feigning becomes the norm in these relationships of acquaintance that kid themselves they are friendships. Inasmuch as these larger and thinner circles of friends are a product of a fast pace of life, the corollary is that people have less time for themselves and true intimates; the hours for honesty dwindle and are missed. Taking all four sets of ambiguity together, we can see, therefore, that the attitudes towards friendship inherent in contemporary ethical and social values are themselves part of the problem too. We will come to that.

However, first, this analysis begs a question; have there been times and places in which friendship was not sentimentalised, marginalised or thwarted but rather assessed, valued and supported at the wider, social level? If, as I put it in the introduction, we are denizens of an age in which freedom trounces connection and sentimentality drowns seriousness, did any pre-modern societies have a greater capacity for friendship?

The thought here is not that there might have been periods in the past in which people enjoyed a depth of friendship that we can barely imagine. Such a suggestion would be to indulge in a kind of illusory nostalgia. Nor is it to suggest that certain times were friendlier because friendship somehow burst out all over. (In fact, if friendlier times did exist in ages gone by, we might expect them to be characterised by outbreaks of animosity too, such are the ambiguities of amity; to claim a friend is not much different from declaring another an enemy.) Rather, it is that there may have been societies whose ethical norms, social institutions and moral frameworks were better placed to negotiate the perils to friendship – the pressures associated with utility, sexuality, dissimulation and so on – thereby enabling people to realise friendship's promise more readily. Then, at a social level, friendship was regarded as constitutive of society, not as merely a marginal or bothersome concern.

This is a possibility worth pursuing for what it might say about today. And at a cursory level there is evidence to support it. For one thing, the great philosophers of friendship appear in distinctly historical clusters. Plato, Aristotle and Epicurus wrote within two or three generations of each other and the later Romans Cicero and Seneca, who also devoted time to the subject, did so to recover what they thought was being lost in relation to the Greek take on things. Why is it that not since the Greeks has friendship been thought a problem worthy of a solution, Nietzsche wondered? Perhaps friendship was high on their moral agenda because it was high up in their list of social goods, and not compromised as it is today.

A second age of writing on friendship occurs in the Middle Ages, though it is more silver than golden, and produced the positive philosophies of Thomas Aquinas, Aelred of Rievaulx and Anselm. The rare philosopher of friendship after them, notably Montaigne, writes rather like Cicero and Seneca, in a mood that laments the present and tries to look back.

Evidence of another sort is found if one considers the tales and legends of famous friends; the greatest are located and promoted in the same, distinct periods of history. The stories of Orestes and Pylades, Achilles and Patroclus, and Aristogiton and Harmodius were celebrated in classical times. The stories of Amys and Amylion, Bewick and Graham, and Abelard and Heloise are medieval.

So, given that the weighty reflections on friendship tend to come from certain periods in history, let us consider first the classical era and then the medieval to see whether these were exceptional times, and if so what they reveal about the best social conditions for friendship.

Tyrant slayers

When Pausanias, author of the best-selling *Guide to Greece*, visited the Athenian agora in the second century CE he saw a remarkable statue. It depicted two friends, Harmodius and Aristogiton. They stood next to each other, striding forward with arms raised and hands clutching daggers. An image of a friendship was located at the political heart of Athens.

Six centuries earlier, at the time the friends had lived, Athens was in the grip of a dynastic tyranny established by Pisistratus and inherited by his sons Hippias and Hipparchus. The beginning of the end for the dictators came when Aristogiton slew Hipparchus – the act the statue commemorated. In fact, the friends were probably motivated more by personal passion than revolutionary fervour. According to Thucydides, Hipparchus was in love with Harmodius and was close to forcing Harmodius to return his love. When he insulted Harmodius' sister instead, the friends decided to act and kill his brother Hippias.

The date they chose was the feast of the Panathenasa in July 514 BCE since on that day citizens could bear arms in the city without rousing suspicion. They told a few others of the plan; their job was to foment a more general revolt in the chaos that would follow the deed. But when the friends saw one of their fellow conspirators talking to Hippias they panicked, thinking that they were betrayed. Full of fury, they switched targets and rushed off to find Hipparchus whom they killed. Harmodius died in the fight and Aristogiton was captured, tortured and then executed. The tyrannicides had apparently failed, though as it turned out they had destabilised Hippias' hold on power. Four years later the dictatorship was over and he was expelled from Athens.

The statue was remarkable because the original, made by the master sculptor Antenor, was the first public monument in Athens commemorating mortals, not gods. This anthropocentric shift was prompted by the high esteem which Harmodius and Aristogiton rapidly assumed; they came to be regarded as the founding heroes of Athenian democracy. Legend quickly mixed in with the event itself. Herodotus records how Hipparchus had been warned of his doom in a dream. A tall and beautiful man stood over his bed and murmured: 'O lion, endure the unendurable with enduring heart; No man does wrong and shall not pay the penalty'. When Athens was later sacked by the Persians, and Xerxes carried the original statue off to Susa, the Athenians commissioned a replacement immediately they returned to their city as if to secure the liberty of the place. 'Truly a great light shone in Athens when Aristogiton and Harmodius slew Hippias', sang Simonides of Ceos, getting his history slightly wrong. The two were symbolically embraced in the songs that were sung at symposia. Indeed, the friends were celebrated more than Cleisthenes, the man whose reforms secured Athenian democracy more surely than anything they did.

To enquire into the form and function of classical friendship is to enter contested territory. Scholars of the highest calibre radically disagree. Statues aside, the bulk of the evidence rests on surviving texts which immediately raises a problem. The Greek for friend, *philos*, has at least as wide a range of associations as its English equivalent. It can be applied to fellow-citizens as in the Shakespearean invocation, 'Friends, Romans, Countrymen'. Equally it could refer to a friendship of the most intimate kind: 'But if the while I think on thee, dear friend,/All losses are restored and sorrows end' (Sonnet 30). So it is hard to discern whether the use of the word 'friend' in the political sphere denotes merely a kind of patronage or something more personal and intimate. Context alone can decide.

However, context allows us to imagine that one of the reasons why an image of friendship resonated so strongly with the Athenian sense of identity was that the experience of being a citizen was far more closely interwoven with the experience of having friends than it is today, when public and private aspects of life tend to occupy different spheres of existence. To be an ancient Athenian was to be a citizen and to be a citizen was to take part actively in the collective life of the city. For example, it seems that during the periods of democracy, an Athenian's political well-being was for the most part more important to him than his economic well-being. Of course, he had slaves and women to attend to his domestic affairs when he was away exercising the right to vote, sitting on juries or attending staged political events like games and plays. But taking part in the life of the polis was a way to build social standing that neither wealth nor family alone could match. For this reason Democritus describes citizens becoming physically ill when absent from public life. Jacob Burckhardt concludes: 'Life for the citizens of Athens was existence, not business.' Or, as the contemporary historian Christian Meier sums it up: 'Where we today introduce our economic and other interests into politics, the citizens of Cleisthenes' era politicised their own persons.'

Friendship of various sorts therefore assumed a prominent role in public life simply because friends inevitably found themselves engaged in it together. At one level, friends provided support and expected support in return. Xenophon credits Socrates with such a utility-based account of friendship in his *Memoirs of Socrates*; although good friends are to be judged superior to any other possession someone might have, it is in relation to what they give that they are valued, he says. At a less material level, public shows of loyalty were an important characteristic of those one would call friends. The story of Orestes and Pylades is an extreme case in point. As Orestes contemplates killing his mother to avenge his father, Pylades provides the kind of unequivocal, public support that lesser friends would shrink from giving: 'Embrace the enmity of mankind/Rather than be false to the word of heaven,' he advises according to Aeschylus. Resonant aphorisms of the time include, 'Gold can be put to the proof by fire, but goodwill among friends is tested by circumstance', and, 'Reversals test friends'. And a friend would become a foe if they failed to stand by you.

Having said that, there is much less certainty as to the organised role that groups of friends and companions would have played. Some scholars conclude that politics was an exercise of friendship to the extent that friendship itself was a political institution and the basis for factions or parties. More likely, friendship was an element in political activity simply because the number of people involved in politics was relatively small, certainly by today's standards, and citizens could not avoid personal considerations, for good or ill.

Thus, it is quite natural for Aristotle to include a couple of chapters on political constitutions in his discussion of friendship, an inclusion that to the modern mind is something of a non sequitur. As there are three kinds of friendship, he says, so there are three kinds of constitution – in descending order: kingship, aristocracy and timocracy. Friendship and constitution coincide to the extent that both form just communities. So, in the best case, the just and good king thinks of his subjects in the same way that the just and good friend thinks of others. In an aristocracy or timocracy, social goods are assigned according to position or property respectively, in a way that is parallel to utility-based friends who share things. Conversely, when these constitutions collapse into tyranny, oligarchy and democracy, they can be thought of in a way analogous to the collapse of friendship. A tyrant is like someone who considers their own advantage not the advantage of others. An oligarchy keeps things within a closed circle and does not distribute according to merit. And a democracy, though the most friendly of the three, is like friendship stretched to the limit since majority rule inevitably alienates the minorities who do not agree.

Aristotle was also keen to cultivate a kind of civic affection in his political philosophy. After all, he argues, mutual affection is the best reason that people have for wanting to live together, and a happy city-state is one in which people do more than associate with each other merely for commercial reasons or defence. He wants citizens to have a concern for each other's character too in order that they might not only live, but live well. For example, he believes citizens should be proud of fellow nationals who are exemplars in some way, perhaps having won a race at the Olympics. And citizens should be dismayed at unethical behaviour, not just because of the injustice but because it diminishes everyone. This quality of civic connectedness is different to, say, the modern concern for the human rights of others. And it is deeper than, say, the groundswells of sentiment evoked by mass media. The goodwill Aristotle wants people to embrace looks to other citizens' spiritual wellbeing alongside material success, an aspiration that perhaps inevitably reaches beyond the expectations people have (or would want) from a modern plural democracy. Having said that, I do not think he imagines that polity rests on friendship. The fundamental relational institution in the ancient city-state was the household. If living well and happiness originate in friendship and love, these things are mediated through the household into the city at large. In other words, a city in which the community was characterised by a deep mutual concern would be a good breeding ground for friendships. But that does not make the city a collective noun for friends.

One way in which this mediation might work in practice, and where we get closer to something that is in part an institution of friendship that overlaps with politics, is at the Greek symposium. *Symposium* literally means 'drinking together' but these dinner parties were more than occasions when individuals met to feast. Food, drink and entertainment were vehicles that provided common ground for the main purpose of the evening, namely, talk. The alcohol was consumed ritually, for example, in order to steer the participants along the fine line between enough alcohol to loosen the tongue and crack personal reserve, and too much alcohol that reduces conversation to incoherence. Imbibing alcohol was not the only thing that encouraged intimacy. The layout of the room did too with couches facing inwards so that sightlines crossed. The participants also drank out of the same cup, an act with religious overtones that enforced a sense of reciprocity; it was sometimes referred to as a *philotesia* which could be translated as a cup of friendship. Songs were sung. Alongside those that referred to Harmodius and Aristogiton other lines that survive rehearse themes of friendship: 'He who does not betray a man who is his friend has great honour among mortals and gods', goes one (it loses something in translation).

So the symposium was a place in which friendships, alliances, solidarities and comradeship could be forged and fed. Its political dimension was found in the bridge it provided between what we would now think of as the public and private arena. It took place in the privacy of the host's house: if a host invited people he knew from his life as a citizen to a symposium he was also inviting them into his personal life, perhaps for friendship. The gesture is not wholly unlike the difference between going out for dinner with someone or meeting them at a reception, and inviting them to a dinner party at home. The latter carries overtones of friendship that the first may put on hold.

Not that the symposium was necessarily friendly. Enemies could find themselves at the same do too. This was the case at the symposium which we know more about than any other, the one Plato creates in his eponymous dialogue. The host was Agathon, life-long friend and probably lover to (another) Pausanias who was also there. Two other old friends present were Eryximachus and Phaedrus. Their presence is worth noting since, a year after the date on which Plato sets the *Symposium*, they were exiled for the religious crimes of profaning the Eleusian Mysteries and mutilating Herms; they were friends and conspirators. Next to Agathon lay Socrates and during the dinner the philosopher rather belittles his host, perhaps because he had also invited Socrates' archenemy Aristophanes. There was no love lost between them on that night either. The last person to make an appearance, though later on, was Socrates' sometime love interest and sparring partner, Alcibiades. He arrives drunk and then drinks more, showing that the propriety of even a structured occasion like a symposium could be broken.

In summary: ancient friendship appears to have been a kind of third category of relationship, neither wholly private nor wholly public. Quasi-institutions of friendship like the symposium linked the two realms to an extent that does not really exist today. Political philosophers advocated a kind of civic affection on top of the rights and responsibilities of which civics is composed today. And friendship seemed to play a widespread if informal part in the democratic life of individuals simply because politics was highly participatory.

Garden friendship

However, the political expression that friendship enjoyed in classical times did not pass without comment. One of its most prominent critics was Epicurus, who lived a few years after Plato and Aristotle. For him, the city was far from being the place in which people could live well. In fact, he thought it was antithetical to friendship. His point is well summarised by his later follower Philodemus of Gadara:

> If a man were to undertake a systematic enquiry to find out what is most destructive of friendship and most productive of enmity, he would find it in the regime of the polis.

This suspicion of politics can be understood as a reaction to Mediterranean society as it had then become. The city-state had ceased to be the dominant political entity that people identified with as a result of Alexander the Great's conquests. His domain extended across the known world and integrated it to a degree that had not been seen before. However, the empire was not at ease with itself. When Alexander died, his successors divided and fought over it. Epicureanism was in part a reaction to this unrest, preaching a retreat from 'the prison of affairs and politics'. Instead, Epicurus took to his philosophical school which he called the Garden (a deliberate antonym to 'city') and although we know relatively little about it, because only fragments of texts survive, he clearly cultivated a philosophical way of life founded on the friendships that he believed could only flourish in that context.

Another critique of political friendship comes from Plato. In the *Republic*, his dialogue on justice that includes a kind of blueprint for an ideal city-state, he notably excludes friendship as a political force. Instead personal relationships of a different sort come to the fore, namely, those of family. Plato suggests that people within the city, and certainly among the ruling classes, should think of themselves as belonging to one big family, to such a degree that they share wives and children and think in exactly the same way on any issues that confront them. The advantage of such an extreme sense of collective identity is that if people regard each other as brothers, sisters, fathers, mothers, sons, daughters, ancestors or descendents, the city will be protected from its worst fate, being divided and torn apart. On this criterion, friendship does not fair well since its exclusive nature can nurture dissent, division and even dissidence.

One might ask how Plato can espouse this view and the apparently opposite attitude he has towards friendship in the *Symposium*. It is most likely that he is deliberately exploring different ways of looking at things; perhaps he has the treachery of Eryximachus and Phaedrus or the antagonism of Socrates and Aristophanes in mind when he sidelines friendship in the ideal polis.

In fact, he takes a different stance on friendship in the city again when he broaches the subject in the *Laws*. This work is generally taken to be an attempt at an applied political philosophy, as opposed to an idealised one. The description of friendship it presents seems to resonate closely with the way friendship most likely functioned in ancient Athens. For example, in the *Laws* friendship is regarded as a valuable not dangerous social force since it makes for the happiness of citizens. Legislators are urged to keep 'friendship in view' in the decisions they make, for the sake of supporting civic cohesion. Citizens are similarly encouraged to value the services of their friends more than their own services to others, an attitude conducive to civic affection.

The *Laws* also sounds notes of realism. Plato advises, for example, that friendship between a master and a slave is inherently impossible no matter what good intentions either may have. In a similar vein, he deals with ambiguous aspects of friendship. Friends know each other well, he observes: this means that a good friend might testify to another's virtuous conduct in order that the city can reward them aright; but it also means that someone will know enough to reveal a friend's corrupt finances or political shenanigans should that be necessary, betraying the friendship in the name of civic justice.

The end of an age

If we leap forward three centuries and into the Italy of the late Roman republic, it seems that friendship again had a more public role than today. Although politics was limited in scope, having nothing to do with the economy and little to do with social matters like education or religion, the aristocratic classes participated extensively in politics not least because many public offices were held for only short periods of time and thus required a large supply of candidates. Thus, in a way different from Athenian democracy, late Roman republicanism was highly participatory for the ruling classes and encouraged circles of what the Romans usually called 'clients', again a category within which friendship would inevitably exist on occasion and thereby gain public standing.

Coupled to this, the great political events of the day, typically battles in court, were publicly staged and could attract very widespread attention; a defendant would call on friends as witnesses and clients to side with him in the crowd. Of course, these displays of amity were not necessarily notable for the longevity of their loyalty or intimacy. An opponent with bigger pockets, greater charisma or other winning ways could conjure 'friends' as needs required. Cicero, for example, remarked more than once that he longed to see his true friend Atticus because he was sick to the back teeth of the cloying affection of 'these politicking and powdered-up friendships'. However although Romans could be sceptical about political friendship, they were not merely cynical about it in the way Disraeli implied when he commented that there are no permanent friends in politics, only permanent interests. In fact, public abuses of friendship could have serious repercussions for someone's political standing to an extent that is, again, hard to imagine given the private nature of friendship today.

Probably the best example of this is Cicero's *Second Philippic*, a defence of himself against the accusation that he had violated the friendship of Mark Anthony, lover of Cleopatra. The story goes that after the death of Julius Caesar, Anthony had plans to succeed him, which the republican Cicero resisted in a speech to the senate on 2 September 44 BCE. A furious Anthony counter-attacked a couple of weeks later, casting aspersions upon Cicero's loyalty. Cicero replied by writing a pamphlet – the *Second Philippic* – though on the advice of Atticus it was not published until after his death.

The argument is complex but basically turns the accusation around: he counter-accuses Anthony of betraying their friendship, having calculated that no-one would support his claim to be Caesar's successor unless he had publicly become Cicero's enemy. To support his case, Cicero lists other ways in which Anthony betrayed him. He says Anthony had read aloud private letters that Cicero had sent him, an act that destroys the relationship between distant friends (and one that backfired since, if Anthony sought to prove Cicero's enmity, the letters were full of goodwill). Not that goodwill exists now: Cicero is quite willing to fling mud at his erstwhile friend, accusing Anthony of winning people's loyalty by inviting them into his bedroom, among other things. However, the point here is not the mire of late republican politics. It is to show that the obligations of personal friendship carried weight in public discourse and that breaches of friendship could count severely against someone at a political level. What is more, if an individual was accused of such a betrayal, they would not brush it off as tittle-tattle or leave it to the diary pages, but would go to great lengths to restore their virtue even when the original affection was clearly long gone.

Then again, although political friendship was still an important notion to be defended, in Cicero's mind at least, it was also one that was being eroded in his times. This is shown in a more systematic defence of friendship he wrote in the same year as his confrontation with Anthony. It is in the form of a dialogue, with the main speaker as one Gaius Laelius, a Stoic philosopher born a hundred years before Cicero, a literary device which perhaps signals that Cicero knew he did not have any particularly new ideas on the subject though they needed repeating for the sake of his times. Which he did well:

> Friendship is ... complete sympathy in all matters of importance, plus goodwill and affection, and I am inclined to think that with the exception of wisdom, the gods have given nothing finer to men than this.

He believes it springs from nature rather than need, citing the association of animals as proof and pointing out that people who enjoy good friendships are relatively self-sufficient to start with. He also clearly has the ambiguities of friendship in mind – 'in friendship there can be no element of show or pretence; everything in it is honest and spontaneous' – and the subtleties of political friendships which are examined in some depth:

> The most important thing in friendship is the preservation of a right attitude toward our inferiors.
>
> It is incumbent upon those who are the superiors among friends or relatives to avoid making any invidious distinctions between themselves and their inferiors ... similarly it is incumbent upon the inferiors not to take umbrage at the fact that others surpass them in natural endowments, fortune or rank.

That Cicero dwells on relationships between individuals of different social standing is more proof, first, that these relationships counted for something in Roman life and, second, that Cicero was alarmed at the way political amity was eroding. Hence throughout the dialogue there is the sense that friendship is under threat because of events as much as because it demands fine balances. That his argument is tinged with nostalgia and set in the past, recalling a 'truly remarkable friendship' between Laelius and Publius Scipio, is another indicator. As is Laelius' talk of 'deadly perils' overhanging friendship. Further, echoing his argument with Anthony, Cicero is keen to assert that loyalty to a friend should not include having to bear arms against the state, as good a sign of troubled times as any. It is ironic that the tyrannicidal atmosphere of Cicero's day placed such stresses upon public friendships, whereas one of the most enduring public images of friendship for the Greeks was of two tyrannicides.

Cicero was right to be concerned. The horizontal politics of the republic were replaced by the vertical government of empire and with the rise of imperial Rome came the demise of these forms of political friendship. Roman society became highly stratified under the emperor, obliterating aristocratic participation in governance on a large scale along with the matrix of friends, clients (and enemies) that overlaid it. Public relationships were clouded by the tensions between the senate and the emperors, with sincerity compromised by deference, goodwill by distrust, and loyalty by obsequiousness. The political virtues of friendship ceased to carry their praiseworthy value; individual interests became permanent. So, although one should be wary of summarising these changes and their impact in a few lines, it does seem right to highlight a certain privatisation of friendship that stemmed from the newfound danger associated with its public expression.

Evidence for this is found in two epistles that Seneca, the tutor of Nero, wrote in 63–65 CE just over a hundred years after Cicero. One, entitled, 'On Grief for Lost Friends', pretty much speaks for itself. Seneca himself was well acquainted with grief; he was nearly executed by Caligula, banished by Claudius, and finally ordered to commit suicide by Nero. In the epistle he argues that grief for a friend is either self-indulgent, a kind of phoney proof to ourselves or others that we truly loved the deceased, or, more sadly and perhaps more appositely for Seneca, it is a sign that someone has no other friends left, or no candidates for new ones.

In the second epistle, 'On Philosophy and Friendship', he picks up on Cicero's belief that people have friends out of nature not need but takes this self-sufficiency to extremes that again seem to reflect on his times. First, he argues that the virtuous person can do without friends, though he may not wish to, the implication being that many have to nonetheless. Second, he says that friends offer a way of exercising noble qualities; again, the implication is that ignoble times do not afford many opportunities for public displays of friendship. Third, he adds that friendships which are made for their own sake, and not for an individual's advantage, insulate people from the full effects of bad fortune. And again, it is in bad times that such a reflection makes most sense. Moreover, Seneca argues that winning friends is a matter of will not luck. 'Just as Phidias, if he loses a statue, can straightway carve another, even so our master in the art of making friendships can fill the place of a friend he has lost.' One does wonder what quality of friendship is possible under such circumstances? The golden age of friendship, such as it was, is well and truly over by Seneca's time.

There is a more positive side to these changes. For example, when operating mainly in the private sphere, the range of individuals one might count as friends seems to have been extended. In another letter, Seneca compliments one Lucilius for living on friendly terms with his slaves. They are unpretentious friends, Seneca says, fellow-slaves as far as fortune is concerned:

> That is why I smile at those who think it degrading for a man to dine with his slave. But why should they think it degrading? It is only because purse-proud etiquette surrounds a householder at his dinner with a mob of standing slaves.

Aristotle would have been astonished at this, as he would at the suggestion that husbands and wives might think of themselves as equal friends too. Plutarch, for example, writing about the same time as Seneca, outlines three forms of marriage in his *Marriage Precepts*. The first is purely sexual. The second purely contractual. However, the third and best type is one of total unity between husband and wife who are bound together by love; their marriage is like 'a rope of intertwining strands'. Plutarch implies this has less value than friendship between men, but it is clear that the combination of warmth and strength that this model of marriage implies could not last long unless embedded in a reciprocal friendship.

Again, this marks a discernable change of emphasis from the philosophical models of friendship in ancient Athens. For Aristotle, the ideal relationship between husband and wife is one of affection but it is determined by the 'natural' superiority of the man over the woman. He likens it to the relationship between rulers and subjects in an aristocratic constitution. The man rules and only gives over to his wife those parts of life that are 'fitting' for her, parts of life that seem pretty limited. If she rules over the household because she inherited it, for example, Aristotle says that is like the degenerate form of aristocratic constitution, an oligarchy not based on excellence but power. Aristotle is surely right that friendship will be limited between someone who is owned, like a slave, and their owner.

All in all, political friendship of the sort that could hold such weight in Greek times, unravelled in the late Roman republic and early period of empire, and has never really achieved the same degree of traction since. A number of changes took place: levels of active citizenship were seemingly permanently reduced (something that the invention of the modern professional politician perpetuates being a representative, as opposed to participatory, democracy); quasi-institutions of friendship like the symposium went into demise; the aspiration that citizenship should include an affectionate concern for one another's wellbeing, not just a disinterested exchange of material goods, came to an end. Of course, friendship was thought by some to be problematic, even undesirable, in the political sphere. The point, though, was that it had to be discussed. So it is no surprise that the greatest age of philosophical writing on friendship is Greek, with an attempt to revive it in the late Roman republic. In the sense that every citizen had a political existence that provided a public framework within which friendships could grow, these were indeed times more open to friendship.

Public kisses

So what of the second period in which there is a marked philosophical interest in friendship, namely, the 'silver age' of the Middle Ages? Something different is going on here, I think. Friendship carried a degree of social impact as a result of two factors. First, certain activities like eating and sleeping that are today carried out in private then had a distinctly public dimension, notably in relation to the household. This leant a corresponding degree of social importance to the friendships that could accrue around doing these things together. Second, a strain of religious piety that put a high value on friendship developed during the Middle Ages which when coupled to the flexibility that existed within the institution of the household also contributed a significant social dimension to friendship. This religious piety never quite gained the status of religious orthodoxy, though it got close in the work of Thomas Aquinas. However, at a popular level it informed an attitude towards friendship and even a semi-institutionalisation of such relationships that is quite remarkable when compared with today.

I am wholly indebted to the work of the late historian Alan Bray in my description of this period. His posthumous book entitled *The Friend* may well prove to be one of the most important books on the subject for many years. He identifies a tipping point for this move from medieval to modern social attitudes towards friendship in the second half of the seventeenth century. His story begins in the first half of that century and the memoirs of one Sir Anthony Weldon.

In his memoir Weldon describes a farewell. It was between the King, James I, and the Earl of Somerset, Robert Carr, and took place on the staircase of the King's hunting lodge at Royston, Hertfordshire, in the autumn of 1615. The farewell was marked by an apparently deep display of affection. Weldon records the Earl kissing the King's hand and the King hanging about his neck 'slabbering his cheeks' and saying 'For God's sake when shall I see thee again? On my soul, I shall neither eat nor sleep until you come again.' In fact, the exchange was particularly noted by Weldon because he thought the King's farewell an act; Carr fell out of favour at court almost as soon as they had parted. However, this is precisely what makes it so interesting for us.

Given that it was an act, it is wrong to interpret the exchange as that of two friends lost in the spontaneous signs and sentiments of overwhelming affection: public embraces and declarations that eating and sleeping will cease until reunited again were not indicative of some nascent sexual ambiguity or excess of affection, as we who now show reserve with public kisses (let alone sleeping together) might imagine. Rather the King was performing gestures of social patronage, protection and loyalty. Carr, and those who looked on, would have taken them as signs of the King's connection with him but not necessarily affection for him. More generally, the physical intimacies of kissing and eating and sleeping together were symbolic of what we might call social capital; Francis Bacon called it 'countenance' and others 'honour'.

Now, although countenance and honour did not primarily depend on personal friendship, they did not exclude it either. Between James I and Robert Carr it seems there was little love in the autumn of 1615 (and hence for us, the primary meaning of the exchanges stands out). However, if the parties were friends too, then such practices could indeed be tokens of affection. This is the opportunity for friendship: it could then gain some social, as opposed to purely personal, standing.

Consider the significance of these signs in their own right. The kiss is perhaps the most demonstrative but it is not primarily a kiss of affection, as we might exchange kisses on cheeks today. Rather, it needs to be seen in the light of the kiss of peace at the Eucharist. This was a sacramental part of the Mass. When the priests 'shared the peace' with the people, they greeted one another with a kiss as a sign of the union of the Trinity that Christian people sacramentally participated in too. This same kiss in the social setting expresses a reality that says 'we are connected'. It may or may not express a narrower sentiment and add 'I am fond of you'.

Eating and sleeping were similarly signs of social connection, and not mere emotion. Take the eating. The common table was placed at the symbolic heart of the medieval household. It was a place in which everyone from lord to serf ate, each in an allotted place that reflected the obligations of their relationship with superiors and inferiors. The great halls and high tables of university colleges are the legacy of that tradition though they do not quite capture the full significance of the sign. Eating together was not just a representation of pre-existing social relationships. Communal eating constituted those relationships in the same way that the food which was eaten changed into the bodies of those who ate it. To be called up higher was to be called into a deeper connection. And if that included friendship, that friendship was given a corresponding boost in its social standing too.

Similarly with sleeping together. People used to share the same (very large) beds, whence the origins of the epithet 'bedfellow' which means ally or associate, or sleeping on pallets in the same room. To do so was a sign of social proximity. John Evelyn, the seventeenth-century diarist friendly with Margaret Godolphin, celebrates the time that he had 'a private audience with his Majesty in his bed-chamber'; it was the pinnacle of his countenance at Court. But once again, being bedfellows might not be just a sign of social standing. If it also included friendship, that friendship then carried the social weight of the bed, as it were. So, the seventeenth-century Archbishop of Canterbury, William Laud, dreamt of again sharing his bed with the Duke of Buckingham because he longed for his friendship.

Clearly, this symbolic world is long gone. In fact, it disappeared rather quickly – hence the tipping point in the second half of the seventeenth century. The question Bray poses is why it disintegrated to such a degree that the meaning of kissing, eating and sleeping together became unintelligible, even scandalous, just a hundred or so years later?

He does not believe that the cause was a sudden fear of homosexuality. Although 'sodomites' did come to be persecuted with a vengeance around this time, that was a product of the change: as these signs lost their social intelligibility, the idea spread that anyone might be a pervert whereas before the sodomite had been a strange, alien creature, and certainly nothing to do with the unashamed signs of connection.

Another possible cause might be the changes that took place in the layout of houses. This had the effect of moving what had taken place in public into private quarters: servants moved off pallets and into dormitories; grand staircases became back stairs; great halls in which gentlemen served food to all became private dining rooms attended on by servants. These changes were certainly noticed. Visitors from abroad, such as François de la Rochefoucauld, were surprised by them since they had not yet been seen on the European continent. Others, like the French writer and popular orator the Comte de Mirabeau, were surprised that Englishmen had ceased to greet each other with a kiss and used instead a strange shaking of the hand. But again, these are products of change not causes of change.

Bray believes that the fundamental cause is to be located in the way the life of the body itself changed. A whole range of bodily activities including eating, drinking, toilet and sleeping stopped taking place inside what might broadly be called the space of the household and started taking place within the much narrower confines of what we now call the marital space. As a result, bodily intimacy ceased to be an instrument that could be used to carry wider social meanings, including friendship, and came to be associated primarily with the more limited concerns of married couples.

In other words, the public institution of the household was replaced by the private institution of the family. In the seventeenth century and before, people lived in a multiplicity of families and fraternities according to their status, their age, their work or their luck. It is important to remember the high rates of death in childbirth too which meant that husbands might often marry several times and that children could be routinely raised by a number of different people including stepparents, relations or friends. These various connections were held together by the fundamental unit of society, the household, which in turn created lots of space for friendship to play an important social role.

One gets an alternative feel for the role the household played at this time in the work of another contemporary historian, John Bossy. He has also charted the changes in the West over this period and notes, for example, that in the latter Middle Ages fraternities were hugely popular, the product of a widespread desire to share formalised friendships that went beyond the limitations of kinship and the hierarchical structures of feudalism. Celebratory meals and affectionate greetings did not only allow individuals to bond alongside family and fiefdom but also served to mitigate the civil unrest that might follow within the household at the breakdown of particular friendships.

It is also within this context that the relationship between John Evelyn and Margaret Godolphin can be understood. These two Restoration figures had an extraordinary passionate and chaste friendship in spite of the fact that Evelyn was married. John, Margaret and his wife Mary did on occasion experience uncertainties and jealousies, as the quote from her letter at the start of Chapter 2 shows. But to the modern mind it is remarkable that, first, John and Margaret could associate so freely in and around London without rousing suspicion and, second, that Mary could come to count Margaret as her friend too and write the following to her husband:

> She is now yours in spirit and the bond of friendship as she is mine, and how can I be happier? ... you both want something of each other, and I of you both, and I hope in God we shall all be the better for one another, and that this three-fold cord shall never be broken.

What happened in the seventeenth century is that these notions of household collapsed. Social ties and solidarities were replaced with marital bonds and the boundaries of the family; the threefold cord was replaced with a tie, for two. Physical intimacies that were part of the public, symbolic world of friendship, in particular kissing and sleeping together, came to be seen as the prerogative of husband and wife, excluding friendship in the process. Incidentally, this also explains the rise of homophobia. The meaning of affectionate connection between men was undone and, if subsequently displayed, was left hanging undecided. The world had changed and with it a public space within which friendship could flourish largely disappeared too: it was relegated to the strictly private.

Another way of looking at this is to consider how the meaning of the word 'society' changed over the same period. The older meaning is simply being together. To say, 'I enjoy your society' was to say 'I enjoy being with you'. Friendship could be a form of society. But during the seventeenth century, society came to carry structural and organisational overtones too, as in civil society or industrial society, meanings that eventually became dominant and marginalised the friendly dimensions. The philosopher John Locke is seminal in this evolution of the word. His 1690 publication *Essay concerning the True Original, Extent, and End of Civil Government* is instructive. In Chapter VII, 'Of Political or Civil Society', he discusses what he takes to be the origins of what he calls civil society: 'The first society was between man and wife, which gave beginning to that between parents and children, to which, in time, that between master and servant came to be added.' In other words, he takes what he sees as the first society of Adam and Eve, in the Bible, and uses that as a model for civil society as a whole.

Note the binary structure – man and wife, parents and children, master and servant. One can clearly see the priority being given to what we now call the nuclear family, and the nuclear family as the basis of society to boot. However, that is not the only thing to notice. In turning the 'first society' into a model for 'civil society', he changes the sense of the word society: the first society was company; political society is organisational. It evolves from being something that tangibly exists in the company or companionship of two or more individuals to being an abstraction or framework within which individuals should find a sense of who they are and where they belong. In short, instead of people *having* society, they think of themselves as *in* a Society.

The changes to the marriage laws are a tangible example of the difference. Before Locke, marriages were fixed rather informally between individuals, again part of the pre-modern culture of flexible kinships and friendships. Afterwards, though, marriage changed and could only be contracted after the bureaucratic rituals of reading banns and signing registers, and in the presence of a clergyman (also called a Clerk in Holy Orders). He was the official representative of the new form of Society within which the marriage was explicitly located. So the Lockean move can be thought of as doubly detrimental to friendship. First, it makes a binary notion of family the basis of Society. And second, that Society is conceived of as an ominously bureaucratic entity that has few means of understanding, let alone nurturing, friendship.

Sworn brothers

However, the story does not stop there. The most recent research of historians like Bray is showing that something else was lost in these changes too. It seems that the social standing that friendship could gain by virtue of the more public life of the body was only part of it. Within the same milieu, friendship did not just piggy-back on certain symbolic practices but was semi-institutionalised in its own right. This brings us to the second factor that had a bearing on friendship in the Middle Ages, namely, a widespread religious piety that valued it.

Bray's lead into this really quite surprising dimension of medieval friendship is his research into shared graves. Shared graves, as opposed to common graves, are those in which two people are buried together as an explicit demonstration of the friendship that they shared in life. Once you start looking for them, Bray notes, they start appearing everywhere – in churchyards, crypts, cathedrals and chapels.

Consider, for example, the fourteenth-century monument above the tomb of Sir William Neville and Sir John Clanvowe: it could not be missed in the church of the Dominicans in Constantinople. These two English knights died in 1391 and what is remarkable about their funerary monument is the way that their shields, which are carved on it, incline towards each other. Similarly, the crowns of their helmets meet as if in a kiss. These heraldic arms show that Sir William and Sir John were in life what was known as 'sworn brothers', a voluntary form of kinship based upon an exchanged promise of committed friendship.

These kind of sworn brotherhoods were afforded great respect in premodern Europe. They existed alongside marriage – there is no evidence that they were exclusive relationships – and were even tacitly sanctioned by the Church; the kiss of the helmets shown in Constantinople is the kiss of peace from the Mass, the sign of divinely sanctioned connection. In the West, a kiss of peace exchanged before receiving communion together was in fact the action that sealed the sworn brotherhood. Sir William and Sir John went to such a Mass and made such a commitment in their youths. In Eastern Orthodox Christianity, copies of prayers that were specifically written for the creation of sworn brothers and sisters survive to this day.

Sworn brotherhoods existed up to the seventeenth century. Another example, in the chapel of Christ's College, Cambridge, is the grave of John Finch and Thomas Baines from 1682. It is topped with a single flaming funerary urn that represents the mingling of their remains. The inscription reads:

> So that they who while living had mingled their interests, fortunes, counsels, nay rather souls, might in the same manner, in death, at last mingle their sacred ashes.

Another reflection of the popularity of the ideals of such sworn friendships is Jeremy Taylor's *Discourse of Friendship*. When it was published in 1657, it was reprinted several times in quick succession. He wrote:

> The more we love, the better we are and the greater our friendships are; let them be dear and let them be perfect ... it would be well if you could love and if you benefit all mankind; for I conceive that [heaven] is the sum of all friendships.

In fact, there is further evidence that friendships were sworn between women too and right into the nineteenth century, though less frequently and less publicly; the new society could not eradicate it entirely. The famous friendship between Anne Lister and Ann Walker, recorded in enormous detail in the diary of Anne Lister, was one such. Bray believes that this is what Lister was referring to when she confided in her aunt that she and Walker had decided to settle as companions for life in a friendship that 'would be as good as marriage'. On Easter Sunday, 1834, they solemnised this commitment by receiving communion together in a church near York Minster. 'I had prayed that our union might be happy', she wrote. In other words, although their sworn friendship did not command the social significance that it might have done up to one hundred years before, the old religious forms of making a 'promise of mutual faith' were still available. Lister does not explain in her diary why they received communion together. She did not need to. That is a question for us.

The piety of friendship

So how are we to understand the philosophy or rather theology of friendship that underpins this action? This is where the element of religious piety comes in. During the medieval period, a number of Christian writers had reflected upon the importance of friendship in the monastic setting. Consider first the writings of Anselm, the sometime Abbot of Bec and Archbishop of Canterbury who died in 1109. He is often remembered today for his 'proof' of the existence of God (it is widely discredited now but roughly runs that God must exist because to exist is the greatest possession anyone can have, so God, of all beings, must have it). But when not proving God's existence, Anselm was a prolific letter writer to his monastic brethren. It is these letters that provide us with his thoughts on friendship.

What is notable about them is an extravagant use of, again, apparently affectionate terms: 'eye to eye, kiss for kiss, embrace for embrace', he signed off one. As between James I and Robert Carr, this kind of language is easily misunderstood and it is wrong to read it as sexual. Anselm's kisses are the same expression of connection, this time sealed by the monastic setting – a literal union of monks linked by their monastic vows and communal life. The extravagance of the language is an expression of the extravagant reward their commitment will bring them, the everlasting joys of Heaven.

In fact, and not unlike like James I and Robert Carr, it is possible that Anselm was not primarily thinking of human affection at all in these terms of spiritual endearment, strange as that may seem. When in 1093 he moved from Bec to Canterbury, many of his brothers suspected that he did so with little real regard for them as individuals. Anselm did not want the job, not because he would miss his friends but mostly because of the dangers it would bring him. When he left, his friends wondered whether his friendship with them was actually more to do with the hope of what is to come, rather than the pleasure of what is now.

Anselm's theology of friendship is esoteric: his high religious friendship was extended only to his monastic peers and even then there are grounds for thinking that he was drawn to a piety of spiritual connection that tended to diminish the friendships themselves. This is what changes with Aelred of Rievaulx; the two elements fuse together. He was born in the year Anselm died and at the age of 37 was elected abbot of Rievaulx, a monastery of some 300 Cistercian monks, the remains of which stand to this day outside Thirsk in Yorkshire. His great work on friendship, *Spiritual Friendship*, was written soon after he arrived at Rievaulx. It is inspired by Cicero: if Cicero had written an account of friendship addressed to the late Roman republic, Aelred wanted to do the same for a Christian society. However, he is innovative too. Several things stand out.

First, he argues that friends should be willing to die for each other. His model in this respect is the life of Jesus: 'A man can have no greater love than to lay down his life for his friends', as the writer of John's Gospel has it. This saying has been co-opted today to express the sacrifice made by soldiers in war but in John's Gospel it means something rather different. It is actually a comment on the demands of discipleship. Earlier in John's Gospel Jesus says that he does not call his disciples servants but friends. Why? 'I call you friends because I have made known to you everything I have learnt from my Father'. In other words, the friends of Jesus both understand who he is and are prepared to pay the price of living by that conviction – even to the point of death. It is for this reason that 'friend' was almost a synonym for 'Christian' in the early, persecuted Church. Aelred implies the same should be true in his time.

Other things that Aelred thinks should be typical of friends follow from this. The love between friends should be undying in the sense that 'he that is a friend loves at all times'. Even if someone is unjustly accused, injured, cast into flames or crucified in ways that implicate their friends (as was the case for Jesus), the friendship should not cease or else it was 'never true friendship'.

Third, Aelred thinks that friends should share all things in common. This was a pattern of behaviour that was established in the very earliest days of the Church and is recorded in the Bible in the Acts of the Apostles. In Aelred's vision of friendship, sharing things in common comes to represent how friends are other selves to each other: 'And the multitude of believers had but one heart and one soul; neither did anyone say that aught was his own, but all things were common unto them.'

Conversely, Aelred is suspicious of lesser kinds of friendship, such as Aristotle's friendships of utility and pleasure. He believed that people either share true friendship or carnal friendship, the latter seeking worldly pleasures or material gains (sex and utilitarian advantage as I have described them here) and not love of another human being. Part of the reason for this rather harsh stance is that Aelred is very conscious of what he would call original sin: after the fall of Adam and Eve love 'cooled' and a range of evils including avarice, envy, contention, emulations and hates made inroads into love and 'corrupted the splendour of friendship'. It would be hard to beat such a summary of the ambiguities of friendship! At the same time, Aelred did not think that such ambiguities should be taken as to the detriment of friendship per se. Rather, they are themselves a reflection of his high doctrine of friendship: he thought that friendship appeared first in the Garden of Eden, and so, although fallen friendship is certainly fallen, it is also a remembrance of the paradisiacal time that was. Moreover, he goes so far as to hold that God is friendship, like Thomas Aquinas. So a friend is a guardian of heavenly love and friendship is a taste of paradise:

> Come now, beloved, open your heart, and pour into these friendly ears whatsoever you will, and let us accept gracefully the boon of this place, time, and leisure.

It used to be thought that Aelred's writings on friendship were a romantic vision of friendship within the cloister. But it now seems that his account of friendship lent itself to popular piety – in much the same way as the beatitudes in the Sermon on the Mount might today: it was an ideal that Jesus himself embodied and touched on aspirations that many people might have: it was readily conveyed in biblical stories and so was readily accessible. Thus, many people, not just monks, developed a devotion to their friends that they interpreted through Aelred and incorporated into their spiritual life.

That, in turn, is behind the phenomenon of shared graves and sworn friendship. For Augustine, the death of a friend provoked a profound personal and theological crisis. But for Aelred, the death of a friend (something, incidentally, that he also experienced) was the culmination of love, witnessed to by the love that lives on in the heart of the surviving friend. For all the agony of mourning, the death of a friend is an experience of eternity in the present. As Cicero put it, 'Even when he is dead, he is still alive.' Friendship's greatest gift is, thus, that it lifts the veil between this world and the next and provides a foretaste of the everlasting love of heaven here and now.

It is in this context that shared graves and the rites of sworn friendship in the Mass make sense. The shared grave is not just a private, romantic gesture of friendship at the end of two lives. It is the natural, final resting place of friends whose commitment in this world was both their ideal, amidst the difficult demands of relating to others, and hope, as a foretaste of the love to be shared in eternity. Similarly, sharing the kiss of peace and receiving communion together was symbolic of the ethic that shaped their relationship with each other, their obligations to others, and ultimately their faith in God.

So seeing friendship within this Christian frame is not to paint it in pietistic gloss. Rather it adds a new dimension to the practice of friendship that builds on the advantages afforded it by the social conventions of pre-modern society. Friendship could not only become attached to various public demonstrations of connection, and so gain some public standing. It could achieve a semi-institutionalised status that far from being exceptional was part of a wider social order that many people understood and warmed too, whether or not they were sworn friends themselves. Again then: in the sense that the Middle Ages provided a social space within which friendships could be nurtured, we can see that it too was more open to friendship and indeed that friendship was constitutive of society.

Clearly the issue of what has been lost since needs to be pursued further: that is a matter for the next chapter. However, before we come to that, there is one more twist to add to the tale of sworn friendships. I mentioned the friendship of Anne Lister and Ann Walker: the savvy reader may be pondering two things that are significant about it. The first I have already referred to, namely, that their friendship existed in the nineteenth century, 100 years after the tipping point when conventions changed; how can this be? The second is the one thing that anyone who has read about Lister and Walker knows: their friendship was sexual. So again, how could they take advantage of this form of friendship to secure their union when even suspicion of the sexual element could have branded them as sinners?

The two things are connected. For one thing, although social conventions changed, the reason sworn friendship was not eradicated entirely is that religious pieties are not easily dislodged: friendship may have stopped carrying much social weight but that does not mean the sentiments that lay behind sworn friendship were abated. This meant, in turn, that although sworn friendships disappeared from view, that could be an advantage to those like Lister and Walker who both wished to celebrate their love in valid symbols, and did not want to draw too much attention to it, because it contained a sexual element.

In fact, Lister and Walker were not buried together. Anne died of a fever in Georgia after their 15-month journey together across Europe in 1840. As Bray suggests, it is significant that the other Ann did not leave her body there but went to the enormous lengths of having it returned to Halifax and buried in the church where they made their vows. Walker no doubt intended to be buried there alongside her – not just as a gesture of love and grief, but as the final and culminating act of their friendship.

6
Politics of Friendship

Every real friendship is a sort of secession, even a rebellion.

C. S. Lewis

The final frame of Ridley Scott's movie *Thelma and Louise* is frozen: it holds a '66 Thunderbird car in midair above the Grand Canyon, lit brightly in orange pink sunshine. Thelma and Louise are in it. Behind and above them in patrol vehicles and helicopters are the massed ranks of the police who have chased them across the state. The two women are seconds from certain death. And yet just before they flew over the edge, they warmly embraced and smiled: 'You're a good friend', Thelma said, to which Louise replied, 'You too, sweetie, the best.' In other words, to see them only as about to die is to miss the moment. They are actually going to their freedom – the eternity of the final frozen frame. It captures the high point in their lives and their friendship has brought them to it.

The friendship of these two women who were tired of being victimised by men is evident from the opening scenes of the film. Thelma, played by Geena Davis, and Louise, played by Susan Sarandon, clearly know each other better than their respective husband and boyfriend know them. Their sense of one another is knit together to the extent that they can be critical of each other without ever questioning their bond. 'Friends share everything in common,' noted Plato. They have shared the road, a rape, a robbery and rude truck-drivers. It has brought them to that point high in the air. So what is it about their very modern friendship that finds its culmination in a glorious and defiant suicide?

The answer is a politics of friendship that might be said to have begun to take shape in the very different time and place of Anne Lister and Ann Walker (that Thelma and Louise's '66 Thunderbird becomes a 'shared grave' is particularly evocative). Lister and Walker loved each other and borrowed the rites and sentiments of a form of friendship that used to be regarded as a pious celebration of two people's connection to make a commitment. That such sworn friendship had mostly disappeared in the nineteenth century in which they lived was convenient: it could be used to express the seriousness of their intent without having to seek the blessing of a society that would not give it. But their act was not just one of convenience.

Relationships like theirs were becoming suspect and so they inevitably assumed a political edge too. Lister and Walker probably thought of their sworn friendship as a kind of resistance; a way of quietly defying a society that sought to keep women and friendship in check. But a few years later such personal resistance had developed, first, into a form of public protest which by the end of the twentieth century had, second, evolved again into acts of creative politics. It was as if the disappearance of the semi-institutional commitment of friends as part of the make-up of society made way for the reappearance of friendship as an important driving force behind the demands of people who sometimes quietly, sometimes militantly, sought recognition and respect because they found themselves at odds with it. In short, committed friendship had done a complete about turn: its constitutive role had become subversive – the means of circumventing social norms that would outlaw its love.

Suffragette city

The women's groups who fought for suffrage in the nineteenth and early part of the twentieth centuries provide a focus for the first turning point, from personal resistance to public protest. Friendship here becomes a relationship from which individuals find resources to refuse oppressive social conventions.

For a long time, suffragettes found little support within the corridors of power. Their public protests were often met with annoyed bemusement, even in circles that might be thought sympathetic. One newspaper of the time, *The Referee* (which carried the laudable strapline 'The paper that makes you think'), reports an incident in June 1914 that is typical. A liberal demonstration at Denmark Hill in South London was being addressed by David Lloyd George, who was to become British prime minister. These liberals, though, were far from tolerant of women's demands. 'At the outset Lloyd George had to submit to a

Suffragist interruption', the paper reports, 'but the interrupters were quickly chased away from the scene.' There followed a series of 'extraordinary scenes' including one Revd Mr Wills being seized 'by people in the crowd and thrown into the pond at the back of the grounds of Bessemer House'.

When he got out he came to blows with the man who pushed him in, and Mr Wills was very roughly handled. Another male sympathiser followed the reverend gentleman into the pond, and a Suffragette had a lot of her clothing torn off. The stewards were helpless in preventing the public from maltreating the interrupters.

Little wonder, then, that friendship was an important source of solidarity and succour amongst these women and their relatively few supporters.

The record of one friendship in particular has survived the passage of time and provides further details of how they functioned in this milieu. It was between two 'Ultras' (so-called because they were radical even for suffragettes), Elizabeth Cady Stanton and Susan B. Anthony.

These celebrated women are of about equal ages, but of the most opposite characteristics, and illustrate the theory of counterparts in affection by entertaining for each other a friendship of extraordinary strength. Mrs. Stanton is a fine writer, but a poor executant; Miss Anthony is a thorough manager, but a poor writer ... To describe them critically, I ought to say that opposite though they may be, each does not so much supplement the other's deficiencies as augment the other's eccentricities. Thus they often stimulate each other's aggressiveness and at the same time diminish each other's discretion.

Stanton and Anthony met in May 1851, the early days of the American women's movement before the Civil War. They were both already leading lights within it and their meeting was fortuitous: the Ultras were moving into the 'collective action stage', as Michael Farrell calls it in his book *Collaborative Circles*. Stanton and Anthony's friendship was central to this gearing up for battle and by the end of that first summer they had become close friends: Anthony stayed at Stanton's for much of July and August where she quickly became known as Aunt Susan to Stanton's several children. Thereafter their relationship could even be said to have been marriage-like in certain ways, though not sexual. For example, Stanton ensured that there was a room for Anthony permanently at the ready for when she came to stay.

Their friendship flourished on a number of levels. One was personal. For example, Stanton describes how she and Anthony comforted each other when other members of the group wanted to tone down their fiery proclamations.

> For Miss Anthony and myself, the English language had no words strong enough to express the indignation we felt in view of the prolonged injustice to women. We found, however, that after expressing ourselves in the most vehement manner, and thus in a measure giving our feelings an outlet, we were reconciled to issue the documents at last in milder terms.

Another level was practical. Stanton had family commitments to juggle with her political engagements and could not devote as much time to travelling and speaking as Anthony. In contrast, Anthony felt inadequate in writing speeches. So their friendship enabled them to divide the labour. Anthony would do much of the research for the speeches, and Stanton would come up with the drafts: 'She supplied the facts and statistics, I the philosophy and rhetoric, and together we have made arguments that have stood unshaken by the storms of thirty long years ... the united products of our two brains.'

But the friendship was also important at a political level. For example, together they devised a programme of annual conventions at which participants gave speeches and read poems: the women realised that this mode of political action was effective both in terms of developing their philosophy and in terms of presenting women in different public roles (contemporary newspaper reports express surprise that women are actually as good at oratory as men). The friendship was also a forum to discuss their experiments in how to dress and behave in public. Similarly, they talked about how women could set their own agenda in the pursuit of happiness, something that had hitherto been the prerogative of men. All in all, their friendship was a private powerhouse driving a public, political way of life.

Having said that, politics also cast a shadow over it on occasion. For example, Anthony never married and whilst her collaboration with Stanton was for the most part premised on accommodating the responsibilities Stanton had for her family, Anthony did sometimes object: 'Woman must take to her soul a purpose and then make circumstances conform to this purpose, instead of forever singing the refrain, if and if and if!', she once argued in an implicit criticism of the compromises that marriage necessitates. But, it was actually the married Stanton whose mature politics did more to challenge their friendship towards the end.

Her final speech to the National American Woman Suffrage Association in 1892, entitled 'The Solitude of the Self' and often regarded as her masterpiece, was premised on an existential philosophy that implicitly marginalised friendship. In the speech, Stanton laid out an argument which said that women cannot depend on men because ultimately everyone is alone. This made a good case for suffrage because, if true, everyone must be allowed whatever means are available in society to guard themselves against such isolation. Stanton invoked the figure of Robinson Crusoe to demonstrate her case. He was an individual who lived in a world of his own, who was arbiter of his own destiny, and who used every faculty at his disposal to ensure his own safety and happiness. So, Stanton argued, should a woman be. She deployed the figure of Crusoe's companion, Friday, in her analogy; every woman would have her own woman, a Friday, she said. But what at first reads like an invocation of the early days of her friendship with Anthony turned out to distance them from each other, because she concluded that whilst a Friday brought benefits, ultimately no-one could rely on anyone apart from themselves. The implication was that even Anthony had left her alone at certain moments:

> In youth our most bitter disappointments, our brightest hopes and ambitions, are known only to ourselves. Even our friendship and our love we never fully share with another ... Alone a woman goes to the gates of death to give life to every man that is born into the world; no one can share her fears, no one can mitigate her pangs; and if her sorrow is greater than she can bear, alone she passes beyond the gates into the vast unknown ... how few the burdens that one soul can bear for another!

Michael Farrell believes that this was Stanton's public 'divorce' of Anthony and that for what remained of her life she wanted to be independent of her. When, for example, Stanton's husband died, Anthony invited her to move in with her and form a new 'home for single women'. Stanton refused. Even close friends of forty years standing are never far from the unpredictable ambivalences of friendship.

As far as I know, Stanton and Anthony's friendship was never itself a source of public comment. Neither was it at the time interpreted, or meant, as an act of rebellion against the world of men (as if, for example, its marriage-like characteristics were a judgement on the bonds of real marriage within which women may have felt themselves to be trapped). In other words, the friendship fired a challenge to society but was not perceived as an affront in itself. But if we move forward a few years, to the feminist movement of the mid- to late twentieth century, then the politics of friendship takes its second step forward, now itself becoming a form of protest. By this time, both contemporary and reconstructed historic friendships between women could be seen as acts of emancipation in their own right.

Political weight

A good example of this interpretation of friendship is found in Lillian Faderman's *Surpassing the Love of Men* – a study of women's friendships in the Victorian period whose title alone says much (in the Bible it is the love of David and Jonathan whose love 'surpasses that of women'). She examines what she calls romantic friendships between women such as Emily Dickinson and Sue Gilbert, and finds them surprisingly common. However, Faderman's purpose in recovering these stories is not only historical. It is political and becomes explicit when in a provocative move (and no doubt with a wry smile on her face) she classifies them as lesbian. Not that she means they were necessarily sexual. In fact, she believes that is an uninteresting question. Rather, she uses the word lesbian to emphasise the social and political power of 'women on women' friendship that she wants to draw attention to within the context of the feminist politics of her time: 'a lesbian is a woman who makes women prime in her life, who gives her energies and her commitment to other women rather than to men', she explains.

This classification is not wholly anachronistic. Lesbianism has long been a trope for subversive women regardless of their sexual proclivities. For example, in the Victorian writer Algernon Swinburne's posthumously published novel, *Lesbia Brandon*, he connects the high intellect and independent spirit of his lead female character to an 'inevitable' lesbianism, and indeed 'inevitable' eventual suicide. It is also the case that as the friendships Faderman documents blossomed, so they came to be regarded with anxiety, raising almost ridiculous concerns, such as the possibility that they might cease wanting to marry. However, it is only in relation to contemporary feminism that such friendships can be made to carry the political weight of being seen as positively subversive. As Simone de Beauvoir observed in 1949, 'often women choose to become lesbians when they are absorbed in ambitious projects of their own, or when they simply want liberty and decline to abdicate in favour of another human being as the hetero-sexual relationship generally demands of females'. Faderman's goal is the same; to make an explicit link between the very fact of being friends and female emancipation. As she concludes:

> Many of the relationships that [men] condemned had little to do with sexual expression. It was rather that love between women, coupled with their emerging freedom, might conceivably bring about the overthrow of heterosexuality – which has meant not only sex between men and women but patriarchal culture, male domi-nance and female subservience.

So how is it that friendship itself comes to be thought of as an act of rebellion, as opposed to just providing support for certain kinds of protest or, going further back to the times of Walker and Lister, merely being an act of personal resistance? It stems in large part from the cri-tique of society that feminists have put forward: friendship is seen as an embodiment of that critique. This embraces a number of aspects. But take one.

As many feminists see it, many of the problems of the modern world arise from the dominance of individualism; the fact that being human is thought of in terms of being a 'social atom'. This is the same social atomism at the heart of post-Kantian ethics, though let us now frame it in a different way. Think of the model of human individuality that is often referred to as 'rational economic man' [*sic*]. According to this model, individuals make decisions according to the maxim of max-imising things for themselves, and themselves alone. Rational econ-omic man views work as a place where he should gain as many advantages for himself as he can; he competes against his peers or competitors and balances out the pain of working hard (and reaping rewards) and the pleasure of an easy life (with few prospects). Alternatively, he views his political acts as a way to maximise the benefits he receives from society; he votes for whoever promises to improve health care, to create more jobs, and not to raise taxes. More mundanely, when he travels he seeks to maximise the speed with which he can get somewhere; he pits his need to travel fast against other road-users' desire to do the same. All in all, decisions are taken primarily with himself in mind. Any consideration of others is judged by the disadvantage, inconvenience or pain such an action would cause to him. He operates as a social atom.

Now, of course, rational economic man does not exist in reality. Even the most selfish individual has family and friends who they care about, at least some of the time: they will do favours for a colleague at work; will make allowances for a slow pedestrian crossing the road; will consider various policies when voting; a man may even shop for his wife. As Thomas Aquinas might have said, even egoism can reach out to others. However, the point about the model of a rational economic man is that the modern market economy favours behaviour that is like his. It is a competitive environment, driven by maximising utility, vying for scare resources, and encouraging predominantly instrumental, utility-based relationships. The net result is that behaving like rational economic individuals tends to be reinforced – in everything from government policy to the size of pay packets – and behaviour that is not like it tends to be marginalised.

Many thinkers, not just feminists, are unsettled by the implications of this. What they have in common is objecting to a conception of individuality based upon social atomism, and preferring instead an idea of people acting according to their attachments. Communitarianism is one alternative model. It is a way of thinking about socio-economic behaviour based upon the belief that people make decisions about their actions in terms of their social, not individual, identity. As Alasdair MacIntyre puts it:

> I am someone's son or daughter, someone else's cousin or uncle; I am a citizen of this or that city, a member of this or that guild or profession; I belong to this clan, that tribe, this nation ... These are the given of my life, my moral starting point.

The problem with communitarianism for feminists is that although it takes people's attachments seriously, it can be blind to the possibility that these attachments may be oppressive. For example, if a woman is treated harshly by her husband or a person of colour is ostracised in a predominantly white workplace then communitarianism could inadvertently legitimise that abuse by celebrating the family connection or professional association regardless of the details. Communitarians can, of course, share the values that abhors exploitation of this kind. But what critics of communitarianism argue is that it risks sidelining those values in the effort to shake off social atomism; valorising social networks like family, school, church or nation can validate the relationships out of which injustice can grow by taking them as 'the given' of life.

Right relationship

One feminist response to the inadequacy of alternatives like communitarianism has been to emphasise the necessity of choice in relationships. And this is where friendship as a model of social connection comes in because it is a relationship that is, in large part, characterised by voluntarism. Marilyn Friedman has written suggestively about this. Friendship, she argues, is a good way of thinking about what it is to be connected, particularly in the urban context in which many forms of connection are based on choice not obligation. Her point is not that friendship encourages people to have a friendly attitude towards each other which in turn reduces incidents of abuse: that would clearly be highly unlikely, to say nothing of the fact that cities can also be places of isolation, loneliness and alienation. Neither does she treat friendship idealistically, as if she were describing a society of friends in which division, dissent and disruption had ceased: we have seen that friendship has little to do with utopias. Rather, she focuses on friendship to outline a way of engaging with society.

First, it promotes networks of support. In the urban context, this is manifested in the way that cities are home to all sorts of minorities. The city provides both the anonymity that allows someone to separate themselves from their oppressive origins and the networks around which to form common interest groups to resist that oppression. In bars and clubs, community centres and meeting rooms – 'amongst friends' – individuals can reinvent themselves without having to deal with the intolerance of crabby families or insular neighbours. Second, whilst such friendships may be politically passive, the city makes it highly likely that at least some people within these groups will become politically active – either fighting for their own interests or expressing solidarity with others. This is where the political dynamic kicks in: friendship gains the social and political weight and comes to be seen as an act of emancipation itself.

Another feminist thinker, Mary E. Hunt, develops this thought. For women, she argues, friendship is the context within which the political imperatives of mutuality, equality and reciprocity are best experienced. This is empowering at the personal level and becomes political because, as relational 'experts in the field', it gives women things to teach the world around them. In terms of the argument against individualism, what women's friendships teach is what she calls 'right relationship' – exemplified in a balance of four elements. The first is love, feeling more united than separated. The second is power, the power to fight for the right to choose what is best. The third is embodiment, the struggle to love ourselves and each other particularly in relation to our bodies. And the fourth is what she calls spirituality, the sense of being concerned for quality of life. When friendships manifest such right relationships they become both liberative and witnesses to it.

Hunt realises that friendship has its weaknesses stemming from the ambiguities inherent in it. These may well stymie the attempt to find the right balance she seeks; such are the contingencies and vulnerabilities of being human. However, she concludes that when friendship is regarded as the norm, it reflects values that are different from those associated with social atomism and, indeed, alternative patterns of relatedness that may conceal injustices. This carries with it the potential for much social good. (We might also add at this point that the same was said of friendships in the workplace, if with less political intent: the dominant mode of relatedness there is individualistic and utilitarian; friendship overcomes that when individuals come to know and love each other for who they are, not what they give.)

Hunt describes these friendships in abstract ideals – as empowered, embodied and so on. But what, we might ask, do they look like in practice? What are the ramifications of holding friendship as the predominant social norm? This is where the politics of friendship moves into what I have identified as its third, creative mode. Here it plays not only a critical role but also an inventive one, of asserting and perhaps devising alternative ways of relating. Hunt's notion of right relationship is certainly part of this. But having examined something of the history of women's relationships in suffragettes and feminism, this is a good point at which to introduce another contemporary source of creative relational politics, namely, that of the friendships between self-identified gay men and women.

What are gay men for?

Consider it first from the gay men's point of view. There are many ways to tell this side of the story and scholars sometimes ferociously debate which is best. However, an interesting place to pick it up is to step back in time again to a particular moment in social history, the birth of the coffee house. During the latter half of the seventeenth century – that pivotal period for the emergence of modern society – several hundred coffee houses opened up in London alone. For a society that had come to consider commercial exchange, not social hierarchy, as its basis, they were places where people could relate as individuals on equal ground. (They spread for very similar reasons in the US, if somewhat later, after the Civil War.) Having said that, they were not in general places for friends to meet. In fact, the rules of politeness that guided behaviour in them preferred people not to be close friends, or at least not to act as such; it was thought that conversation between intimates too easily descended into small talk. Rather, the coffee house was a place where for relatively modest amounts of cash (the price of coffee and possibly an entrance fee) all manner of mostly men could mingle for the serious business of discussing anything from Indian imports and Whigish scandals to German Idealism.

A small number of these coffee houses were called molly houses and they served a particular clientele: a male homosexual subculture with a rather different agenda. They were, in a way, the original 'gay' scene and probably varied in character as much as gay bars do today. Some surviving descriptions of them emphasise the effeminacy of the men who frequented them. This sketch is by Edward Ward from his *Secret History of Clubs*:

> They adopt all the small vanities natural to the feminine sex to such an extent that they try to speak, walk, chatter, shriek and scold as women do, aping them as well in other respects. In a certain tavern in the City, the name of which I will not mention, not wishing to bring the house into disrepute, they hold parties and regular gatherings.

A more 'hard-core' picture comes from Samuel Stevens who was probably an agent for a collective organisation that went by the name of the Societies for the Reformation of Manners:

> I found between 40 and 50 men making love to one another as they called it. Sometimes they would sit in one another's laps, kissing in a lewd manner and using their hands indecently.

These sources were written by individuals who basically disapproved of molly houses. However, it would be a mistake to see them solely as scandalous places in which men met to flounce or frottage. More profoundly, they were the cultural product of a discontent that some men felt about the way their society thought they should be male, particularly in relation to the way they were supposed to relate to other men. As Michael Vasey has put it:

> [T]he male homosexual was now seen as an alternative to the masculine ideal of the culture; the role was becoming available as a social identity for those who were ill at ease with the prevailing

masculine ideal within the culture ... It represented a borrowing of the cultural models for affectionate and sexual behaviour, as well as being a form of ironic criticism of the social order that was hostile to this form of same-sex affection.

In other words, when it came to the question of how men should relate in public, possibilities of affection found themselves ousted by the post-Lockean wariness of activities such as kissing and sleeping together, and molly houses provided 'a cultural counterpoint' to the new social norms. They represented an alternative relational space. Men were affectionate in them, no doubt partly driven by the desire for sex but also by a need to explore intimacies and friendships that were limited elsewhere. It is perhaps only going slightly too far to say that the men who frequented them carried the remembrance of a way of relating between men that might otherwise have been increasingly excluded during this time of social change. If we ask tongue in cheek, what was the significance of these homosexuals to society at large, the answer in a word is friendship.

Lads, blokes and metrosexuals

Leaping to the present day, it is obvious that in many respects ideals of masculinity have shifted again. What is interesting about this, though, is that many aspects of male affection are still tied to notions of what we now call gayness. Take the phenomenon of David Beckham. He has shocked, transfixed and seduced the world because although unquestionably masculine he adopted many of the trappings associated with male homosexuality: his image says many things to men, but partly it says, you can push at gendered boundaries, look beautiful, and even risk public displays of affection. Alternatively, if you consider the return of the kiss as a common public greeting between men, I imagine that in the Anglo-Saxon world at least it has much to do with gay culture: one might also point to other factors such as the love of all things Italian (an association that was once itself a euphemism for homosexuality), but being at ease with physical expressions of affection, gay men have long kissed each other in greeting, and now this has arguably been passed back into society.

When it comes to contemporary attitudes towards male friendship, the evidence is mixed. Negatively, they can be coloured by homophobia, the negative response to the association with gayness. This manifests itself as demonstrable rejections of homosexuality in the

friendship, regardless of whether it is there or not. Think of representa-
tions of men's friendship on television and in the cinema. They can
show male relationships to be stilted and stunted: the men might be
concerned with little more than talking about bedding girls (in *Friends*
think of Joey and Chandler); nailing enemies (this genre of male
friendship reaches back to *Miami Vice*); or straightforwardly deriding
homosexuality (think of B-list war movies and the new recruits sub-
jected to 'pansy-packed' abuse from a sergeant). The point is to display
a conspicuous heterosexuality that negates any suggestion of what
might be construed as affection. This is the tragic side of modern
friendship between men; it means that, culturally speaking, friendship
between men is often trivialised.

More positively, and apart from the increased visibility of gay men
themselves, contemporary culture is willing to explore the more affectionate aspects of male friendship too. It is notable, for example, that
the films of the quintessential all-American hero Tom Cruise routinely
feature his friendships with men. In *Top Gun*, the love that Cruise's
character has for his flying partner exceeds the love that he has for his
female flying instructor, though inevitably the two of them do eventually 'bike off' into the sunset. In Cruise's more recent film *Collateral*,
the only relationship that his character has is with another man,
though it is driven by enmity. More widely, one can observe the emergence of what Mark Simpson has wittily called the metrosexual – a
man who 'consumes in all the best gyms, clubs, shops and hairdressers'
because whether gay, straight or bisexual, his image of his own masculinity allows him to do so. It is no surprise that the narcissistic side
of the metrosexual finds much in common with the self-love inherent
in friendship; as Simpson notes, his sense of self revolves around circles
of friends. Alternatively, he conceives of marriage primarily in terms of
friendship – as opposed to a relationship shaped by prescribed gender
roles – and thinks that tying the knot should be an agreement between
equals: 'the metrosexual is less interested in blood lines, traditions,
family, class, gender than in choosing who they want to be and who
they want to be with'. The male metrosexual also lurks within the
female characters of soaps like *Sex and the City*, in molly house-like
female guise.

However, the extent to which modern man is good at friendship is
debatable. Consider, Yasmina Reza's award winning play *Art*. The plot
revolves around the friendship of three men: Serge who buys a painting of a featureless white canvass at vast expense; Marc who exclaims,
'You paid two hundred thousand francs for this shit'; and Yvan who is

more tolerant and tries to placate them both. The play deals with the fragilities of their friendship which are exposed as a result of the purchase. Marc feels that Serge has betrayed him in what he sees as a pretentious purchase. Serge feels that an unattractive side of Marc is revealed by his attitude to the picture; it shows that he cannot see the difference between financial cost and true value. And they both come to see Yvan's friendship as insubstantial because all he can do as the crisis ensues is all he ever has done – try to make them laugh. In the final scene, Serge and Marc's 15-year friendship appears to come to an end because their masculinity refuses to allow them to admit to each other that they have been hurt. We might say that the friendship does not have the resources to carry them beyond the shock of being honest with one another; the art has exposed their usual habit of shallow friendliness and dissimulation.

Other portrayals of male friendship in novels such as those labelled 'lad-lit' are similarly ambiguous. For example, in Nick Hornby's novels *Fever Pitch* and *High Fidelity*, that tell of the blokeish love of soccer and music records respectively, the male characters flourish insofar as they are companionable with other men, but fail when they try to get close to them. This reflects what the sociologist Graham Allan has found: the dominant images of contemporary masculinity manage to show male sociability but are not so sure when it comes to male intimacy. It seems that male friendship still has its limits. Men are still subject to the dominance of the individualistic and competitive spirit released at the birth of privatising modernity, and an ideal of masculinity that finds affection tricky.

So there is a job for gay men to do yet! What, specifically, might that be for today? Andrew Sullivan is one contemporary writer to have thought about this. His answer focuses precisely on this question of male intimacy. The greatest difference between homosexual and heterosexual men, he thinks, is not to be found in their different sexual attractions or needs, but actually in their ability to sustain friendship. And sustaining friendship beyond the companionability found in football or music, and through the arguments that may break out over a piece of art, is key to the development of intimacy.

The reason for this 'ability' in gay men, Sullivan thinks, stems from the earliest experience of homosexuality. This is not merely one of illicit desire but is one of loneliness: it moves into openness if and only if the gay man finds a true friend, that is, someone who accepts that he is gay. 'Gay men value friendship because until they find their feet as human beings, and let's face it, it's not easy to be 16 and gay, friends are not just friends. They are allies against the world,' was how Tony Warren, creator of the soap *Coronation Street*, put it. So Sullivan's point is not to score points over heterosexuality: 'Gay men have sustained and nourished [friendship] in our culture only by default,' he continues. 'And they are good at friendship not because they are homosexual, but because, in the face of a deep and silent isolation, they are human.'

The job for gay men, then, is to open up closed possibilities of relationship to expansive notions of friendship. In this sense, gay liberation is a potential liberation for everyone:

> It would be to open the heterosexual life – especially the male heterosexual life – to the possibilities of intimacy and support that friendship offers, to vent the family with the fresh air of friendship, to expand the range of relationships and connections that every heterosexual person can achieve.

Having said that, gay men are still men. Their sexuality does not automatically free them from the competitive, evasive and proud features of much modern masculinity. Similarly, their friendship will be marked by the uncertainties, duplicities and confusions of amity (in fact there is an argument that they can develop an exceptional talent for friendly lying because of the need to conceal their sexuality from others). In other words, if there is any creative potential in gay friendship it would be more secure if it rested not just on the humanity of the individuals themselves but on the political impact of their very presence. This is the line of thought that was developed in the final years of his life by the French philosopher, Michel Foucault.

Queer lives

In 1982 Foucault gave an interview to the San Francisco-based magazine *Christopher Street*. In it, he argued that the battle for gay liberation is limited if it is thought of only in terms of gaining certain rights. The problem with merely fighting for rights is that it doesn't necessarily change anything fundamental: rights are extended as people become enfranchised, undoubtedly a good thing, but society itself and the way people think about themselves mostly remains the same. Think of something like the 'right' to go to a gay bar (perhaps construed as a right to freedom of expression). This would certainly be part of a modern, liberal society. But the assertion of the right itself does not address the question of why gay bars are necessary to start with. For this reason, Foucault believed that the success of gay liberation is not just to be measured by the extent to which homosexuals are free to come out and live 'gay lives'. Nor by the extent to which it opens up the heterosexual life. Rather its true goal should be more radical. It should be one that begins a process by which people can find a way out of feeling the need to define themselves according to a particular sexuality at all. What does he mean by that? Think again of the emergence of molly houses and, now, gay bars. The fundamental issue is the negative aspects of the social changes that led to the need for them to start with, which stems in turn from the collapse of the household and the dominance of a modern idea of society: it is this that has consequent ramifications for the way people relate to one another, particularly when it comes to affection. Gay liberation needs, therefore, to find ways of addressing these deeper issues too.

This is undoubtedly more difficult. However, in another interview entitled 'Friendship as a Way of Life', Foucault suggested a way forward when he noted the fact that modern society seems to be especially anxious about the way people behave in it. 'Society and the institutions which frame it have limited the possibility of relationships [to marriage] because a rich relational world would be very complex to manage.' According to this view, the challenge at the heart of gay liberation is the freedom to love, befriend and relate more widely; it is to create or imagine a society in which individuals have more options, one that permits many more possible types of relations to exist.

Now, it might be thought that this is to do with sex. But that is actually, I think, a distraction. What is far more disturbing at the social level is the possibility that same-sex individuals are loving each other. This is the point at which gay men and women present their greatest challenge (because they clearly are loving each other): as Foucault pointed out, when any serious attention is paid to the 'problem' of homosexuality, it rapidly becomes clear that the real problem is that of friendship; modern society has a problem with that.

It is for this reason that friendship, not sexual acts, lies at the heart of several current disputes about homosexuality. For example, it is no coincidence that the 'gay debate' is often at its most fierce in institutions that feel themselves least able to accommodate such love. Consider the question of gays in the military. The difficulty that the Forces have is that they straddle an uncomfortable contradiction when it comes to same-sex friendships. On the one hand, the military must promote them in the camaraderie that may even call on individuals to die for each other. But, on the other hand, it is an institution within which overtly homosexual love is routinely shamed, if not outlawed, for fear of the intense affections that might 'short-circuit' the rules and habits that soldiers are trained to obey. The matter is controversial because of the thought that military relationships are hard enough to police without the complication of actual love.

Alternatively, what of the current uproar in the Anglican Church over homosexuality? In the United States, this has focused on the consecration of the first openly gay man, Gene Robinson, as a bishop in New Hampshire. However the row started before that, with the appointment in the UK of Jeffrey John to the post of Bishop of Reading. He too was openly gay, but in a celibate relationship. In other words, he was neither engaging in 'sexual sin' nor was he going to teach anything that might be regarded as sexually immoral. The difficulty was that his way of life advocated an unconventional form of friendship. The challenge that posed provided quite enough unease for conservatives to leverage and get his appointment withdrawn.

Therein lies the creative iconoclasm of friendship – its contemporary subversiveness. It presents a challenge that is more than just the introduction of another category of partners; the coupledom of the nuclear family could readily embrace more couples. Rather it opens up the far larger matter of how men and women relate to one another:

> [H]ow is it possible for men to be together? To live together, to share their time, their meals, their room, their leisure, their grief, their knowledge, their confidences? What is it, to be 'naked' among men, outside of institutional relations, family, profession and obligatory camaraderie?

(Incidentally, this also shows why the crisis in the church is not merely a product of religious belief: evangelical fundamentalism merely serves to intensify a widespread unease about the changing roles of men and women in contemporary society.)

The significance of gay friendship is, then, that it is a way of life that seeks to be simultaneously innovative and subversive. It embodies a freedom that stems not only from the early experiences of homosexuality but also from the fact that it emerges in spite of attempts to control and manage relationships. The 'advantage' that gay men and women have is in a sense negative: they do not have access to the institutions that others adopt to shape and understand their relationships. They must literally make it up, partly no doubt by imitating marriage, but also by having to transcend contemporary relational constraints within a context of friendship. It might be thought of as a kind of social experiment, a struggle of invention because of the paucity of the received relational imagination, though, perhaps not unlike Lister and Walker, it can find resources in the older ways of friendship that we have examined.

The paradox is that whilst gay men and women are routinely discriminated against in society, the 'experiments' they undertake in their relationships may actually be a rich resource for others to draw on, not least in terms of friendship. Angela Mason, former director of the UK lobby group Stonewall, described it thus:

> My argument is that lesbians and gay men who have been the most sexually stigmatised group within society, who are derided as promiscuous and immoral, may have a contribution to make to a new ethic of personal relationships that is not exclusively based on sexual gratification or demeaning sexual stereotypes.

Foucault captured the experience of the freedom that gay men and women might find in friendship by considering the kind of relationship that can exist between two same-sex individuals of very different age (the age difference emphasises the inaccessibility of conventional institutions for them to model their relationship on, should they want to). 'What code would allow them to communicate?', he pondered:

> They face each other without terms or convenient words, with nothing to assure them about the meaning of the movement that carries them towards each other. They have to invent, from A to Z, a relationship that is still formless, which is friendship: that is to say, the sum of everything through which they can give each other pleasure.

Again, it is important not to romanticise such relationships in the temptation to idealise gayness and friendship. In fact, Foucault's example deliberately discourages that since the freedom that these two individuals might enjoy could as easily become something that is feared; the anxiety of a relationship that is formless, that floats free of any norms to guide it or conventions with which to express it. This is undoubtedly a fear that many gay men and women will have experienced, particularly as they struggle to form long-lasting partnerships. However, it is a fear that is also seen in the reaction that other people can have to relationships like it. The tendency here is to assume that it must be mostly sexual, in the case of the older person, and mostly for some kind of financial benefit, in the case of the younger. What is hard to admit is that it may be a friendship, one that overturns conventional ideas about physical beauty or material gain (or, to put it another way, one that manages to negotiate certain ambiguities of friendship). Being open to the possibility that it may be genuinely affectionate, mutual, faithful and companionable is for many too much to stomach.

Of course the possibilities represented by friendship depend to a degree upon the success that the individuals may or may not be able to make of it. However, the alternative way of life that they can embody is both a personal and a social opportunity. As Foucault summarises:

> Homosexuality is an historic occasion to re-open affective and relational [possibilities], not so much through the intrinsic qualities of the homosexual, but due to the biases against the position he occupies; in a certain sense diagonal lines that he can trace in the social fabric permit him to make these [possibilities] visible.

Sociological evidence

So much for the theory. What about the practice? The sociologist Jeffrey Weeks headed up a team that researched gay relationships, or as they called them same-sex intimacies. They interviewed people in a variety of such non-traditional relationships, and found that the 1990s saw a growing acceptance of same-sex partnerships, and to a lesser extent parenting, which was in turn reflected in changes in the meaning of family. Within these wider social shifts, they also identified the emergence of a complex but durable friendship ethic. In fact, friendship was the most common way that the interviewees identified their relationships. 'Friendships particularly flourish when overarching identities are fragmented in periods of rapid social change, or at turning points in people's lives, or when lives are lived at odds with social norms,' Weeks writes. The friendship ethic he uncovered exhibits a number of characteristics that I think demonstrate the creative political potential of friendship.

On one level, it has much to do with simply being gay in a hostile world. For example, Weeks identifies a role for the friendship ethic in supporting the individual through what he calls 'fateful moments' in homosexual experience. The significance of friendship in this case is its necessity for survival and self-actualisation in a hostile world (family and other institutions of belonging won't do and may in fact be associated with the hostility). This might manifest itself in a number of ways. Many of the interviewees said that being able to talk frankly about sexual experiences with certain individuals was what distinguished them as close friends. A related factor is the permanence of close friends, or at least an assumption that they will be permanent: 'In contrast to the vagaries of one-to-one relationships, friends ... are a focus of long-lasting engagement, trust and commitment.'

Alternatively, he draws attention to aspects of the relationships he examined that are key simply because friendship itself is highly valued. For example, they are regarded as freely chosen, though many social factors limit the choice in practice; they take time to form; they come in many shapes and sizes running from mere acquaintances to those thought of as family; and they must be 'constantly negotiated and renegotiated if friendships are to work and survive'. (This last issue points to another facet of the weight of its freedom: friendships are not socially legitimised like relationships of kin, and so gay men and women who depend upon them must finds ways of strengthening them and making them stand up.)

However, it is in relation to Aids – another 'fateful' factor – that the friendships perhaps most clearly show the potential for innovative forms of relationship. Aids is a catalyst for extended notions of family because traditional family members are often absent or not able to cope with the crisis. Alternatively, Aids deepens the friendship ethic because of the way it impacts attitudes towards care, responsibility and respect:

> Care involves an active concern for the lives, hopes, needs and potentialities of others. It is a highly gendered activity in western culture, seen typically as the prerogative of women. But from our evidence, it is as likely to occur in male as it is female non-heterosexual relationships ... Responsibility as a voluntary act, revealing our response to the needs, latent or explicit, of others, and receiving in return the responsible behaviour of others, is a clearly expressed ideal of our interviewees. Respect, for one's individual autonomy, and for the dignity of others, is a motivating force of many of the friendship circles of our interviewees. These are all features of the friendship ethic at its best.

Weeks also highlights a common concept amongst those he talked to which he calls the 'good friend' – friendship based upon values such as sharing, support, openness, interests, trust and commitment. His interviewees realise that the good friend may be hard to realise in practice. But what is notable is that they are also alert to trying to strike the right balance that makes for it, the balance between being useful and feeling used, sexual possessiveness and individual autonomy, distance and involvement, choice and obligation – that is, they are aware of negotiating the perils of friendship and realising its promise.

Of course, homosexuality does not necessary make for successful let alone innovative forms of friendship. As Weeks notes, circles of homosexual friends can be as insular and conventional as any other. Moreover, some may fear the freedom associated with being gay and use friendship as a refuge from the personal ramifications of being homosexual, reinforcing social stereotypes rather than encouraging experimentation. In terms of Foucault's analysis, this is a ghettoised form of friendship that preserves, not dissolves, the homosexual identity. But in general, Weeks is optimistic about the significance of the gay friendship ethic for the relational landscape of the early twenty-first century.

Friendship in other relationships

Gay men and women have no intrinsic monopoly on these political possibilities: they are not the only individuals against which society is biased. Friendship between people of different race, creed or class may well represent relationships with which a majority are uneasy and which therefore have social significance. Moreover, non-institutional but committed ways of relating have become widespread in Western societies and these in turn present certain challenges to relationships that are set within a traditional frame.

Anthony Giddens, for example, has coined the term 'pure relationship' to identify not just a type of relationship but a common characteristic of perhaps most modern relationships: 'It refers to a situation where a social relation is entered into for its own sake, for what can be derived by each person from a sustained association with another.' He believes that the pure relationship has arisen because the social function of marriage has changed: it is no longer required to secure the future population but has become an option in the enactment of romantic love. The pure relationship is also a product of a social change in which people value an integrity in their relationships based upon trust, an attitude which makes the older economic necessities that underpinned traditional marriage seem outdated if not repugnant. As Foucault might have put it, the pure relationship has arisen in part because society has impoverished relational institutions: couples may not want to marry for many complex reasons but a perception that the institution is moribund is one of them.

Giddens only mentions friendship in passing in his work, perhaps aware that it is a notoriously difficult relationship for sociologists to define. Indeed, it seems to me that the pure relationship is not necessarily synonymous with friendship. For example, the pure relationship's association with romantic notions of love may actually scupper the evolution of deeper kinds of friendship. If the romantic enactment of marriage is focused on a possessive notion of union – two becoming one – then friendship may be compromised; friendship requires a recognition of the distance as well as the proximity of another self. At the same time, the freedom associated with the pure relationship and the fact that it is entered into for its own sake may provide fertile grounds for friendship; the focus here is not on union but on loving someone for whom they are, which according to Aristotle is the essence of friendships of the highest kind.

Two other sociologists, Liz Spencer and Ray Pahl, have addressed the question of friendship in modern relationships head on. In part, what they see is an interpenetration of notions of family and friends in people's 'personal communities', making the point that many do not think of family and friends as polar opposites (as if family consisted solely of given relationships, and friends solely of those who are chosen). Spencer and Pahl interpret this using the idea of suffusion; personal communities that incorporate family relationships and wider circles of friends. The personal communities of some individuals conform to strict definitions of family. But, for others, they may be family-based in the sense that friends come to seem like family, or friend-based in the sense that family relationships are thought of as friends.

The return of trust and civic friendship?

It is against this background that we can return to the question of regaining a sense of trust in friendship. In Chapter 4, I argued that the secular reinterpretation of Christianity's unease with friendship was to regard it as a selfish and particular relationship that operates outside collective ethical concerns. Spencer and Pahl's evidence that suffusions of family and friends are to be found within personal communities implies that this distrust of friendship is misplaced, at least to the extent that some people do rely on friends. To a degree, then, networks of family and friends are part of the informal and perhaps hidden fabric of an admittedly changing society already: the implication for ethics is that friendship needs to be brought in from the cold.

Against this, though, is the modern politics of friendship which whilst not negative in intent – the aim is to vent the family not undermine it, to extend the ways people love not limit them – is premised on a subversive philosophy that is discontent with the status quo. This may well fuel the sense of distrust in friendship since for all that friendship is critical at a personal level, it may be viewed as destabilising society as a whole. The alarm that feminist and queer ideas can generate is obvious. Alternatively, a conservative point of view will see the spread of Gidden's pure relationship, for example, as wilfully not liberated, a notion that is, say, detrimental to the raising of children who require commitment beyond the couple's own interests, not relationships entered into for their own sake.

A similar uneasiness is reflected in the appropriation of friendship at the civic level. The question here is what kind of impression friendship is making at the socio-political level, given that it is re-emerging as an active factor within social relations? In short, is the politics of friendship reaching into contemporary civil and democratic life? This question can be broken down into two parts. The first is to ask whether private friendship is again achieving an institutionalised form?

The answer, in short, is no. Even though modern individuals may think of their marriages as founded primarily on friendships, the institution itself has yet to respond. It is in way remarkable, for example, that, for all the liturgical changes embraced by churches, the marriage service still contains no explicit reference to friendship. There must be a reason for that. One can speculate that friendship, with its ambiguities on the one hand and subversive associations on the other, is thought too fragile or fraught to form the fundamental unity of society. Or, to put it in terms of the marginalisation of friendship in ethics, it is still distrusted.

The same thing can be said of the new legislation recognising civil partnerships. They are conceived of in terms of extending the legal benefits of marriage to couples whose personal relationships otherwise miss out. It is true that they are a recognition of the relationships of same-sex citizens – in the words of Jacqui Smith, the British Minister for Equality, 'The Civil Partnership Act sends a clear message that we value and support the contribution committed same-sex couples make to each other and to our society.' However, none of the acts being discussed by various governments is framed in the context of friendship or uses the language of friendship, as far as I know. Rather, civil partnerships are strictly legal entities, no more than contracts. There is not, or at least not yet, a new institution of friendship.

The second way in which friendship may be making an impression at the socio-political level concerns civic friendship. This is a more difficult thing to assess. At one level, it is clear that there is such a thing as civic friendliness. One only needs to think of the wide variety of charities and NGOs that are concerned with the quality of people's lives. They work, in part, by promoting networks of concerned individuals, from business, government and other organisations like the church. The relationships that evolve out of this civic concern are often based on certain types of friendship and certainly promote friendliness. However, if the analysis of the last two chapters is anything to go by, it seems to me that in the past there has existed what might be called a higher doctrine of civic friendship which contemporary civic partnerships and networks of goodwill do not embody.

First, a brief reminder of what civic friendship has meant. The basis of it was a positive regard for friendship as constitutive of society. For Aristotle, civic friendship was therefore a concern shared between citizens for each others' wellbeing, a result of the city-state nurturing life in two senses. One was the provision of the means for feeding oneself, defending oneself, and so on. The other addressed the deeper aspect of humanity's aspirations as a political animal, namely, that of not only wanting to live, but to live well. This is what he meant by civic friendship: the shared desire in a city-state for the good life.

In the Middle Ages, a different kind of civic friendship obtained. Here, friendship gained a social standing in the institution of sworn friendship. This existed in various forms over a long period of time, and made a link between the personal commitment of two individuals and their public lives. At one level, it provided a complementary set of personal links alongside the web of relations focused on the household, and, at another, it contributed to the formation of medieval society by making for affinities in addition to those of family or fiefdom.

What these two periods of history show is that for civic friendship (in the deeper sense) to flourish, society must be receptive to it. In ancient Greece, that receptiveness was manifest in a highly participatory democracy that was practically concerned with people's ethical lives, not only their welfare; the politics of the theatre mattered as much as providing daily bread. In the Middle Ages, civic friendship found a place because social institutions were inclusive enough to embrace it; marriage and feudal ties were inter-, over- and under-woven with bonds of friendship. This suggests, in turn, that a high doctrine of civic friendship does not enjoy much purchase today. So although abbreviated comments cannot do justice to the full picture, it seems that contemporary, Western society is limited on two critical fronts.

First, modern democracy has rich mechanisms for looking after citizens' wellbeing in an economic sense – that is, life in terms of staying well, staying alive, staying safe. But it flounders when it comes to the kind of wellbeing that Aristotle's civic friendship was a sign of – that is, life as in 'the unexamined life is not worth living'. Possibilities for civic friendship in the full sense are in fact rather squeezed. On the one hand, the success of modern economic life arguably leaves less time for friends and for the higher concerns of civic wellbeing, perhaps even promoting ways of life that can be positively inimical to friendship. As Ray Pahl puts it in an essay entitled 'Friendly Society', for all that some people are looking for friendly families and families of friends, why is it that so many still put the consumption of things over the cultivation of friendship in their pursuit of happiness? On the other hand, although our contemporary cultural life can be rich, it seems that it falls short of the aspirations of the past. Simon Goldhill's *Love, Sex and Tragedy* amply demonstrates the perhaps inevitable 'poverty of cultural ambition' today when set alongside the Great Dionysia of ancient Athens. This 'enabled and fostered participation and self-reflection on the personal, familial, intellectual and political issues of general concern. Where in the public life of Western society could we look for any such equivalent critical and emotional civic engagement?' – though it is hardly surprising that a political culture dominated by management and the market is so lacking.

Second, modern democracy is characterised by a radical separation of the private and the public. For the variety of reasons explored, friendship has come to be seen as a private concern. Hence the reason that when it does infringe on public life, say in terms of challenging ethical or social norms, it is regarded as subversive. This means that though the notion of the family is changing, and new forms of belonging focused on friendship may be gaining ground, friendship has become politically significant only in the limited sense that individuals are seeking legal adjustments that reflect their personal lives. Thus, civil partnerships are not a sign that friendship is being conceived of as either a quasi-Aristotelian contribution to the good life of citizens or as a medieval-like institution of affection-based bonding. Rather politics is being asked to service people's private lives. (It is possible, of course, that framing civil partnerships in terms of rights is a political calculation and that the socio-political impact of recognising such friendships will only emerge over time. However, there is again a gap to be bridged if the emergence of new 'personal communities' is to lead to an increase in civic friendship: unlike times past when civic friendship moved over the personal and public spheres, the social standing of these modern friendships remains focused on the personal. In other words, the contemporary politics of friendship does not unsettle the strict division of public and private and, for good or ill, this has little impact upon civic friendship.)

Another reason that civic friendship struggles today is that on the rare occasions when intimations of it are visible – in the displays of friendship between politicians – it tends, probably rightly, to get a bad press. Consider the political friendship between George W. Bush and Tony Blair. It is widely treated with Disraeli-like scepticism. Even publications like *The Economist*, a keen supporter of Anglo-American relations, has carried pictures of the two on its front cover under the headline, 'Wielders of Mass Deception'. Little room for a positive civic amity there.

Finally, it is also possible that limited notions of civic friendliness are not only all that a large, plural democracy can hope for, but that they are all it *should* hope for. The reason: civic friendship might incur an unacceptable level of social conformity if promulgated on a large scale. The issue here is the dark side of democracy that Aristotle recognised in calling it a deviant constitution. If it can liberate the spirit and encourage participation amongst the masses, it can also turn in on itself when the majority disregards the life of the minority. Similarly, whilst good civic friendship embraces political reflection and social diversity, bad civic friendship rests mostly on hostility to common enemies, as the philosopher Carl Schmitt's politics of friendship shows. As such, more profound notions of civic friendship today could by hijacked by a reactionary social conservatism and the politics of fear. The ambiguities of friendship raise a head again; it is not without some reason that contemporary politics is wary of it.

7
The Spirituality of Friendship

> Of the things which wisdom provides for the blessedness of one's
> whole life, by far the greatest is the possession of friendship.
>
> Epicurus

Spirituality is something of a buzz word. As Jeremy Carrette and
Richard King argue in *Selling Spirituality: the Silent Takeover of Religion*, it
is a concept that, first, has become highly individualised – it's about
'me' and 'my' quality of life – and, second, has been adopted by organisations from car manufacturers to art galleries, with churches laying
claim somewhere in between, whose primary aim is commercial –
increasing audiences and shifting products.

The spirituality of friendship is similarly something to be rather sceptical about, at least at first. If asked what it might mean probably the
most common answer would have to be soul friendship. But the idea
of soul friendship is one almost irredeemably 'taken-over' by maudlin,
marketable associations too. Type 'soul friends' (or even worse 'soulmate') into an internet search engine and some of the most syrupy
aphorisms on friendship will be returned for your edification: 'A soulmate is someone who has locks that fit our keys', 'You are my fire, my
titanic ocean', etc. The search will also throw up hundreds of dating
agencies, websites promoting relationships with 'celebrity soulmates',
and others that proffer advice on things like 'soulmate health'. Such is
the commercial value of the notion that one electronics manufacturer
has named its MP3 music player SoulMate.

The trouble with this sentimental haze and commodification is that
it cheapens an idea of enormous human and philosophical value: the
spirituality of friendship is not something that can simply be ceded to
the market. It must be recovered because, as I hope this chapter will

show, it captures the attitude best able to negotiate the ambiguities of friendship we have discussed, and make friendship nothing less than a way of life.

The first thing to do is to expose the spiritual veneer of the friendship of the marketplace. Consider again, the Aristotelian conception of the friend as another self. The very ambivalence of the phrase is indicative of a characteristic that is key to any significant spirituality of friendship. 'Another self' captures both the intimacy of close friendship in conveying the idea that this friend is another person like yourself; to discover such a person is to discover someone who at least some of the time mirrors your own thoughts, beliefs and feelings – someone with whom the apparently intractable distance between human beings collapses until it is vanishingly small. And the phrase also includes the vital qualifier that, for all the closeness, soul friends still recognise that they are separate individuals. Each is 'an other self' to the other. Unlike Narcissus who looked in the mirror and saw only himself, the source of the delight of soul friends is that they recognise not only themselves but another human being. 'The essence of friendship lies, I suggest, in the exercise of a capacity to perceive, a willingness to respect, and a desire to understand the differences between persons,' said the philosopher Richard Wollheim. Friends may share an intensity of feeling for each other, including joys and sorrows ('I am happy because she is happy', 'I am sad when he is sad'), and successes and failures (they bask in each other's reflected glory, or languish in each other's mistakes). But they never seek to consume each other or fall into a perpetual embrace.

It is this aspect of difference that the spiritual friendship of the marketplace conveniently overlooks (its sentimentalisation of soul friendship arises by conflating it with the union to which romantic love aspires, a trope which commercially plays much better than advocating difference). The difference is illustrated in the way soul friends behave and lovers are portrayed. For example, soul friends' qualified need of each other, in the sense of respecting each others' individuality, means that they do not mind being physically apart for periods of time. Screen lovers, however, spend the whole time that they are apart yearning for the moment when they will be reunited (and when they are together, they are haunted by fears that they may not be together forever). Alternatively, soul friends understand one another to the extent that they trust one another implicitly: when they befriend others, if to a lesser degree, the seeds of jealousy are not sown between them. Screen lovers, though, cannot in general even countenance a wandering eye, detecting betrayal and the promiscuity of desire.

Deep respect. Implicit trust. No distorting neediness. Even a first look at soul friendship shows that it is nothing if not an exceptional state. Aristotle implied that it could only form between certain individuals. He argued that if someone is not at peace with themselves, virtuous in their habits, attitudes and passions, and honestly conscious of their own self-worth, they will not be able to befriend themselves, let alone another. He is surely right. (Incidentally, this rarity of soul friendship does not imply that connection and belonging may not be found in other perhaps more common relationships, just that they are not necessarily of the same quality. For example, many find a tremendous sense of belonging in a partner, others in their families, both representing profound bonds: husbands and wives, boyfriends and girlfriends share a jealous love, and family ties can arguably never be wholly eradicated. The point is that they are not necessarily bonds of friendship – indeed, they may be exploitative or oppressive. To put it another way, friendship is not the fundamental human relationship, though any acquaintance, partnership, association, marriage or relationship of blood or love may to greater or less degrees be friendly. Rather, friendship is something that may grow from them, on occasion perhaps to share features of soul friendship.)

However, whilst Aristotle makes much of friendship in his account of happiness, he ultimately suggests that the best spiritual life anyone can aspire to is contemplative – an *independent* existence that leaves the role of soul friendship somewhat uncertain. So, when asking what it is, and how might it come about, Aristotle is not the best person to ask. Rather we will now turn to two other philosophers who do make much of it. They are Montaigne and Emerson.

Timing and exceptionality

Montaigne is explicit as regards its scarcity. His argument is that because the individuals capable of soul friendship are so rare, then soul friendship itself will be even rarer; a frequency of about once every three centuries was his estimate. Unsurprisingly, he regarded his friendship with La Boëtie as the winning million to one shot, certainly grounds for questioning the low odds he gives everyone else. However, if his estimation does seem exaggerated it also serves a purpose. It highlights the exceptional value of the friendship to him and carries the more general implication not so much that soul friendship is literally rare but that when it does come about it feels to the friends as if it cannot possibly be matched. There is something about such intimacy that seems unique; its worth seems inimitable and hardly communicable to others.

So what then is it? It is not primarily characterised as other kinds of relationships might be, nor as other friendships – say in relation to a project done in common or a passion that is shared. Soul friendship is fundamentally the unrepeatable experience of knowing, and being known, by that one, particular person. Conveying what this is like is as impossible as describing the experience of thinking; it can only be experienced by doing it, by living it. Other people may be able to view and sense some of the effects of soul friendship (which is why it can be confused with falling in love or conflated with sentimental romance). But the only way truly to know of such friendship is from the inside. Montaigne again:

> If you press me to say why I loved him I feel that it cannot be expressed except by replying: 'Because it was him: because it was me'. Mediating this union there was, beyond all my reasoning, beyond all that I can say specifically about it, some inexplicable force of destiny.

However, for all that it felt like a 'force of destiny', the circumstances that provided such fertile grounds for the friendship between Montaigne and La Boëtie are pretty obvious. Happenstance was key to its formation; timing was everything. The fact is that the historical period in which they lived made them natural allies, so it may feel mysterious that one can say something of how it comes about.

Montaigne admits as much when he explains how the two knew of each other before they met. The most obvious aspect of the common ground between them was that they were both committed humanists in an age when to be religiously unorthodox was dangerous. Montaigne was a close associate of the Protestant King of Navarre, who became the Catholic monarch Henri IV when he married Margot de Valois just before the infamous St Bartholomew's Day massacre. Montaigne therefore had many enemies, and prudence in his public pronouncements was nothing short of a matter of life and death. His dedication to the classical author Plutarch, whose *Lives* he called his breviary, could easily have been reason enough for him to be targeted by fanatics. La Boëtie ran similar risks. He was the author of a treatise called *On Willing Slavery*, a controversial analysis of the religious hegemony of the times that led to him being accused of republicanism. So charged was this aspersion that in his essay on their friendship,

Montaigne found it necessary to defend his friend by watering down his republican convictions with assertions of his respect for the Christian laws of the land. Montaigne had read La Boëtie's treatise before they met, and that is how he came to his attention.

When they did meet, it was therefore almost to be expected that they would fall into a friendship based upon the relief of being able to share their passionate nonconformity. Montaigne indicates the joy of having such a confidant when he says, 'not only did I know his mind as well as I knew my own but I would have entrusted myself to him with greater assurance than to myself'. He is not just talking about the emotional trust that existed between them but the trust he placed in someone whose betrayal could have forfeited his life. That possibility, Montaigne says, was as unthinkable between them as killing their own children. He would have been in sympathy with Dante who put Brutus in the lowest circle of Hell for betraying his friend rather than his country.

So circumstance and timing were necessary conditions for the birth of their friendship. But that is true of any friendship: it is not a sufficient condition for the depth of the soul friendship that subsequently emerged. So the third element to add is that their friendship was exceptional not just because they lived in exceptional times but also because they were exceptional individuals: as human beings they met the conditions for close friendship that Aristotle identified. A combination of rare circumstance, timing *and* right individuality is, then, what makes for soul friendship.

There is one final characteristic of soul friendship that Montaigne draws attention to. As it turned out, his friendship with La Boëtie was short lived. La Boëtie died four years after they met. Montaigne experienced his death as a severe loss, though he saw it as a pivotal episode in the transformation of his life too. The relatively brief length of their friendship therefore serves as a final way of interpreting soul friendship's exceptionality: it does not just mean that it may be only for a chosen few, but more importantly that, if it is known, it is an exceptional experience in the context of any life taken as a whole (it might be said that only some friendships have the qualities necessary to exhibit the characteristics of soul friendship, and then only from time to time – rather like the occasions when dissimulation in friendship gives way to moments of truth).

So the story of Montaigne and La Boëtie's friendship draws attention to the various contingencies that must come together for two people to form a soul friendship: character and circumstance in particular make for its exceptionality and inimitability. But even if we think that these conditions allow for such friendship more often than once every 300 years – perhaps interpreting Montaigne's exaggeration as conveying the sense that a lifetime allows only occasional exceptional relationships – they still imply that the friendship enjoyed by most individuals for much of the time will not attain to its lofty heights. In other words, the really difficult question with regards to soul friendship is not what it is and how it comes about: the conditions for its emergence are relatively straightforward, though that does not make it any more likely; it is also pretty clear how it differs from other sorts of friendship, though the experience of soul friendship can only be fully comprehended by soul friends themselves. The harder and perhaps more pressing question for most, much, of the time is quite simply how to live without it!

This was not Montaigne's concern. He thought he'd had it. It was, though, the interest of another essayist of friendship, the American philosopher Ralph Waldo Emerson. He concurred with the basic insight: 'Friendship may be said to require natures so rare and costly, each so well tempered and so happily adapted, and withal so circumstanced, that its satisfaction can very seldom be assured.' He also recognised the dual aspects of a friend as another self: 'Let him not cease an instant to be himself. The only joy I have in his being mine, is that the *not mine* is *mine*.' However, unlike Montaigne, he did not claim to have experienced it in all its fullness. Rather he believed that he could imagine what it is like in some of the best friendships he did have: 'I have never known so high a fellowship as others. I please my imagination more with a circle of god-like men and women variously related to each other and between whom subsists a lofty intelligence.' He does not therefore celebrate the exceptionality of soul friendship as Montaigne does, but seeks instead a more practical, day-by-day account of a life lived in friendship and hoping for the best.

Telling it slant

Emerson belonged to the school of American philosophy called New England Transcendentalism. What these individuals had in common was the conviction that the divine could be discerned in everything, that nature was symbolic of deeper realities, and that strong character was key to throwing off the deceptions of conformity, tradition and mere appearances. Their method was very much one of engagement. They met, published articles and gave speeches in order to progress along what they saw as a kind of spiritual journey, informed by poets and philosophers. Times of solitude were part of this exchange too. Emerson himself lived for many years in a peaceful, rural town outside Boston suitably called Concord.

His essays can be thought of as philosophical sermons (in his early adult life he had been a Unitarian preacher). They are provocative reflections rather than analytical discourses, designed to unsettle, inspire and exhort. Mary Oliver describes their effect well:

> The best use of [them] bends not toward the narrow and the absolute but to the extravagant and the possible. Answers are no part of it; rather it is the opinions, the rhapsodic persuasions, the ingrafted logics, the clues that are to the mind of the reader the possible keys to his own self-quarrels, his own predicament. This is the crux of Emerson, who does not advance straight ahead but wanders to all sides of an issue; who delivers suggestions with a kindly gesture; who opens doors and tells us to look at things for ourselves.

This commentary on his writing is worth quoting because it also conveys his idea of friendship (and we might suppose the attitude he had towards soul friendship: in Emily Dickinson's phrase, it is found 'in circuit'). It rejoices more in opinions, persuasion and clues than in narrow and absolute convictions; it wanders, thinks kindly, and opens doors through which individuals can look together. He devoted one essay solely to friendship, and it too is not merely an abstract account of the characteristics of amity but in its style and approach evokes the dynamics of the friendships he formed within the transcendentalist circle. This is important for the spirituality of friendship that he wants to convey; it is not like a mathematical formula that can be simply read off the page but must be inhabited by the reader.

We can get a sense of that here by coming to the essay via arguably the most famous of Emerson's friendships, the one he shared with Margaret Fuller. They met when Fuller visited the Emerson household for three weeks in the summer of 1836. He was 33 and did not take to her at first, commenting in his journal on her extreme plainness, distracting eye movements and nasal voice. However, her mind won him over: 'She has the quickest apprehension and immediately learned all we knew and had us at her mercy when she pleased to make us laugh. She has noble traits and powers and cannot fail of a permanent success.' Strangely though, their friendship developed an uneasy undercurrent – some have said a fault – that resulted from an imbalance in their affections. He deeply respected her intellect but she was put off by his apparent emotional coolness towards her.

It is easy to read this as some kind of psychological defect in Emerson: he had already remarried once after the death of his first wife, and perhaps feared the affections of another woman. Even so, he did not reject her. Far from it. He invited her to attend meetings of the transcendentalist circle to which she contributed so much that he then asked her to edit their journal *The Dial*. Alternatively, 12 years after their first meeting, Fuller went to Italy: when 2 years later the ship on which she was returning was disastrously hit by a hurricane and wrecked within sight of Fire Island, killing her, Emerson was grief-struck and showed it; he asked that the wreckage be searched for personal effects, though none were found.

His essay on friendship was written before this disaster but expresses his feelings towards her, I think, when he talks of friends in general going to Europe. He admits he will have languid moods and will regret 'the lost literature of your mind, and wish you were by my side again'. He will feel robbed for a while of some joy. However, he is consoled by the thought that he will be repaid later with more and that the spiritual tie he seeks is far stronger than that offered by romantic love and physical proximity. (And anyway, Europe is hardly a destination likely to keep anyone for ever, he thinks, being only an 'old faded garment of dead persons'.) The tragedy is that it was not Europe that stole Fuller from him but the storms of the Atlantic coast. His essay carries lines that almost seem to have foreseen this disaster: 'Ah! Seest thou not, O brother, that thus we part only to meet again on a higher platform, and only be more each other's because we are more our own?' Therefore, it is wrong, I think, to put Emerson's lack of a soul friend down to an inability to connect emotionally. Something more subtle is going on, something about the spirituality of friendship and the very possibility of soul friendship that his essay provokes us to ponder.

Mere friendship

It begins by celebrating the little wells of friendliness that are to be found in many parts of life: 'We have a great deal more kindness than is ever spoken.' This is particularly clear when it comes to the affection individuals routinely show to complete strangers. If, for example, we welcome a stranger into our house, it is possible to show them a wealth of hospitality, conviviality and generosity that we would never have entertained in abstract – and indeed receive back from them the blessing of their acquaintance as a result. However, there are certain conditions attached to this friendliness, for it is quickly scuppered if the stranger oversteps the mark: if he 'intrude[s] his partialities, his definitions, his defects into the conversation, it is all over'. The risk is that affront and then familiarity breed contempt. In other words, though friendliness bathes the human family with 'an element of love like a fine ether', it is also as thin; disturb it with even a slight current of indignity and it disperses like smoke.

Much of the essay characterises such thin friendship, shared between pleasant enough but shallow friends. In fact, Emerson sounds quite Nietzschean to the reader who lives after both. Even relatively good friendships can be buffeted by 'baffled blows', 'sudden, unseasonable apathies', 'epilepsies of wit and of animal spirits', he says. Such subtle antagonisms begin to play on the friendship and turn its 'poetry into stale prose'; 'in the golden hour of friendship we are surprised with shades of suspicion and unbelief'. This can be distressing and in response many are tempted to overestimate even obviously weak friendships. They prefer to be in denial of its pains and disappointments than admit that these and perhaps most friendships are woven of 'cobwebs not cloth', of 'wine and dreams' – not the 'tough fibres of the heart'.

Others aim at the petty benefits of friendship; they are cherry-pickers in the business of friendship, going for the quick wins and low-hanging fruit, rather than waiting for the deeper friendship that 'many summers and many winters must ripen'. In a similarly horticultural vein, Emerson notes that it is only natural to want to pick the beautiful flowers thrown up by the majority of friendships, and to hope that the wiry roots buried in the damp, dark soil of another's character, soul or mind do not come with them. Nature provides another way of analysing this predicament: 'Is it not that the soul puts forth friends as the tree puts forth leaves, and presently, by the germination of new buds, extrudes the old leaf?' Rotation is a law of human relationships as much as a law of nature.

What is the problem with friendship? Why is it in general so readily altered and so rarely simply true? The fundamental reason is again familiar from Nietzsche:

Every man alone is sincere. At the entrance of a second person, hypocrisy begins. We parry and fend the approach of our fellow-man by compliments, by gossip, by amusements, by affairs. We cover up our thought from him under a hundred folds.

Later Emerson adds: 'To most of us society shows not its face and eye, but its side and its back.'

So for friendship to grow into something more, people must first be able to be themselves: 'We must be our own before we can be another's ... There can never be deep peace between two spirits, never mutual respect, until in their dialogue each stands for the whole world.' That this is hard to achieve, as Montaigne pointed out, means that friendship is too often a kind of descent or a compromise: 'What a perpetual disappointment is actual society, even of the virtuous and gifted!' If most friends were to write truly honest letters to each other, Emerson speculates, they would have to confess how often they had failed one another.

If Emerson is majoring on the ambiguity of dissimulation, I suspect that his tone would have been similar if he had considered the ambiguity associated with sexuality (hence I suspect the perception that he was aloof towards Fuller – he sought a friendship not an affair) and the ambiguity that derives from a utility-driven culture (the transcendentalists stood against this, valuing 'useless' things like beauty in nature over and against the commercial milieu of nineteenth-century America). But for all that it might be tempting to derive an overwhelming sense of disappointment towards friendship from this side of his essay, it is not, I think, the reaction that he intended. Emerson did not lose faith in friendship but rather sought to identify what was often compromised in it. His hope is that, in so doing, the superior value of a deeper kind of friendship might become clearer. Such friendship is not of the merely friendly kind, for all that that sociability makes the world pleasant and bearable. Rather, it overcomes the 'thick walls of individual character, relation, age, sex, circumstance'. It is a friendship that deepens lives: 'High thanks I owe you, excellent lovers, who carry out the world for me to new and noble depths, and enlarge the meaning of all my thoughts.'

All in all, Emerson's aim is to derive a positive attitude from the uncertainties of friendship. It is only by entering into the ambiguities of friendship that its higher possibilities may be discerned; it is only then that the weaknesses of character and the contingencies of time that would inhibit it are overcome. His essay is an exercise in sifting the wheat from the chaff, and treating the matter of friendship with what he calls the 'roughest courage'.

'To do without it'

This is good advice: it takes courage to acknowledge that shallower friendships, though pleasant, are only cursory, and that deeper friendships because they are real need not be handled with kid gloves but can cope with the rougher, tougher exchanges of transformative, significant relationships: 'they are not glass threads or frost-work, but the solidest thing we know'. It is also key to a practical spirituality of friendship – 'friendship, like the immortality of the soul, too good to be believed' – to which he is now in a position to turn.

He does not actually use the phrase soul friendship. His transcendentalist language prefers the phrase 'divine friendship', perhaps echoing some of the earlier Christian writers who came to feel that God is friendship. Emerson himself has a pantheistic idea of God. The divine is not above but is found within the people and things around him: 'My friends have come to me unsought. The great God gave them to me', he says. So soul friendship is therefore divine in two senses. First, it shows a god-like honesty of mind. Second, it enjoys a god-like honesty of affection. This is what he imagines soul friendship is like. Consider these aspects in turn.

A god-like honesty of mind exhibits itself as a truthfulness between individuals that is uncompromised and unmediated: 'Who hears me, who understands me, becomes mine, – a possession for all time'; 'A friend is a person with whom I may be sincere. Before him I may think aloud.' It can indeed be characterised as like those rare encounters in which dissimulation, second-guessing what someone wants to hear, and even courtesy for courtesy's sake, are dropped. Then people deal with each other in simplicity and wholeness: 'A friend is a sane man who exercises not my ingenuity, but me.'

In his essay, Emerson does not just stick to lofty phrases but illustrates what he imagines such friendship to be like in practice. This is doubly informative because the occasion he turns to is not with an intimate such as Fuller, but refers unexpectedly back to the time when he was still working as a preacher. He was a minister in the Second Church (Unitarian) in Boston for three years, having graduated from Harvard Divinity School in 1829. He left the church at the age of 29 because he experienced a vocational change of heart: he came to believe that holy communion was not sacramental. Such a theological change profoundly undermines the role of a minister whose vocation revolves around the administration of the sacraments, and unsurprisingly it was not something his congregation readily understood or liked. However, they did respect his forthrightness – his honesty – and it is for this reason that he came to remember the departure as one of friendship: it had been a moment of god-like truthfulness with the congregation (that he shared this with a congregation again underlines his point: as any minister of religion will tell you, concern with things divine is a rarity compared to the daily grind of indulging a congregation's 'whims of religion and philanthropy', as Emerson himself put it). In fact, his congregation did at first think him mad, perhaps linking his apparent loss of faith to the loss of his wife. But as they listened they came to understand him better, a testament to his desire for truthfulness: 'To stand in true relations with men in a false age is worth a fit of insanity, is it not?' It was therefore an intimation of soul friendship.

The second aspect, honesty of affection, must similarly cut through much 'mush of concession'. The ambiguity that causes the difficulty here is that people are tied to each other in all sorts of ways – by blood, pride, fear, hope, money, lust, hate, admiration – but rarely by genuine love. To be able to offer another tenderness as a result of pure love and not some more compromised affection is to achieve a blessed state indeed: 'When a man becomes dear to me I have touched the very goal of fortune.'

Emerson is interesting in the way he chooses to expand on this quality of soul friendship too because he again suggests that it is best glimpsed in utterly practical and perhaps unexpected ways. He says there is something more emotionally honest in friendship with 'ploughboys' and 'tin-peddlers', in the shared frivolity and rides (today we could add friendship in chat rooms or pubs) than there is in a pretence of high friendship with more 'learned acquaintances'. His point is that friendship must plant its feet on the ground 'before it vaults over the moon', and friends must learn to be good citizens to one another before they are 'cherubs'. If they do not then their so-called divine love will risk revealing itself as a token wrapped up in sentimental affection. Such friends exchange gifts, offer loans, pretend at good neighbourliness, and so on, for the benefit it brings them, not in the hope of genuine relationship itself.

By way of illustration, and no doubt recalling its worst excesses, he contemplates that great institution of middle-class friendliness, the dinner party.

Why insist on rash personal relations with your friend? Why go to his house, or know his mother and brother and sisters? Why be visited by him at your own? Are these things material to our covenant? Leave this touch and clawing. Let him be to me a spirit. A message, a thought, a sincerity, a glance from him, I want, but not news, or pottage. I can get politics and chat and neighbourly conveniences from cheaper companions. Should not the society of my friend be to me poetic, pure, universal and great as nature itself?

Nietzsche could not have composed a wittier aphorism when Emerson wrote: 'Are you a friend of your friend's buttons, or of his thought?'

It is almost as if Emerson envisages three broad categories of friendship. One is common, mundane and passing, though warm-hearted, honest (within its own limits) and friendly as a result. Another is rare, 'divine', and demands a searching integrity and immediacy of encounter. This is the sort that may even on occasion be called soul friendship, though more often is experienced in the best moments of good friendship. In between the two lies a third and arguably the worst: friendship that hopes or pretends it is more but ultimately rests on a wish or facade. There is nothing wrong with them per se. And there may be movement between the different types. But it is particularly in admitting to the existence of the third group of friends that the right attitude towards soul friendship is found. The temptation is to think or hope that these ones are more than they are: but fooling yourself of that is actually to plump for less.

This is, therefore, the key to the spirituality of friendship: 'The condition which high friendship demands is the ability to do without it.' Paradoxically, soul friendship is not best sought by striving for it. The best thing to do is, in a sense, to forget it and practise truthfulness instead – honesty in oneself, towards others, and in any friendship that arises. (As truthfulness is something that must be practised and is rarely perfected, this is another way of expressing the rarity of soul friendship.) To put it another way, the best stance to adopt to be open to the potential in friendship is apophatic – to live expectantly though with the expectation that it will never be wholly realised or experienced unalloyed. After all, even Montaigne only had a soul friend for a short while; even he had to reconcile himself to the reality of normal life when La Boëtie died.

This is not so odd or fatalistic as it may first seem. For example, it is very similar to what is often said about happiness: the thing that kills it is wanting it; but living as if happiness were not the goal of life actually makes for it. (Not that such a neat summary makes the actual living any easier.) For many, like Aristotle, happiness is friendship, at least in part, so, in the same way that most people keep faith with happiness when they do not have it, Emerson advocates never losing faith in the highest aspirations of friendship. 'I awoke this morning with devout thanksgiving for my friends, the old and the new,' he writes. And again: 'I chide society, I embrace solitude, and yet I am not so ungrateful as not to see the wise, the lovely and the noble-minded, as from time to time they pass my gate.' This paradox is not meant to decry close friendship. It is designed to provoke a recognition of the everyday limitations of friendship (and ultimately of being human – limitations that are never more keenly felt than in encounters with others) and to develop an ethos, a spirituality of friendship, that makes for the possibility that these limitations may on occasion be overcome.

The brilliance of Emerson's wandering essay is that its oscillations between high ideals and lower reality precisely reflects the possibility of something more in friendship; it mirrors what friendship is like in life. For most of the time friendship exists within the limits of its inherent ambiguities, but sometimes, if only fleetingly, it shows itself to be capable of much more.

A number of Emerson's aphorisms resonate with these moments of transcendence:

> Let him be to thee for ever a sort of beautiful enemy, untamable, devoutly revered, and not a trivial conveniency to be soon out-grown and cast aside.

> [Friendship] treats its object as a god, that it may deify both.

At other times he adopts an eschatological tone to capture the promise:

> Let the soul be assured that somewhere in the universe it should rejoin its friend, and it would be content and cheerful alone for a thousand years.

> The higher the style we demand of friendship, of course the less easy to establish it with flesh and blood ... But a sublime hope cheers ever the faithful heart, that elsewhere, in other regions of the universal power, souls are now acting, enduring and daring, which can love us and which we can love.

> Leave to the diamond its ages to grow, nor expect to accelerate the births of the eternal.

The 'rougher courage' required for this attitude towards friendship is similarly expressed. For example, Emerson can say that he does not fear the times when he is not with a close friend, or the times when such friendship is absent in the relationships he has, because the spiritual nature of the connection once made is no less vivid for not being currently present: 'my relation with them is so pure that we hold by simple affinity'. Alternatively, the long days or moments of relative loneliness, when life is felt to be humdrum and full of longing, should be thought of as preparation for the moment of true friendship: 'Happy is the house that shelters a friend! It might well be built, like a festal bower or arch, to entertain him a single day.' And, Emerson adds, even if the longing for soul friendship is ultimately unrequited, it will still enlarge the soul: 'It never troubles the sun that some of his rays fall wide and vain into ungrateful space, and only a small part on the reflecting planet.'

The spirituality of friendship is therefore dynamic; it moves from below up. It does not posit a high ideal of friendship as if it were merely a goal to achieve, and which if achieved would suggest that the quest was somehow over. Nor does it analyse the 'low' vicissitudes of friendship solely to reveal the shape and extent of the ambiguities that is the stuff of most relationships, and leave it at that. But, on the assumption that all friendships start from below, it suggests a dynamic process of sifting, discernment, patience, personal struggle and gratitude – sometimes moving up, sometimes sliding down – that opens up the possibility for some friendships to aspire to and realise the best.

And when life is lived less than fully – 'I have often had fine fancies about persons which have given me delicious hours; but the joy ends in the day; it yields no fruit. Thought is not born of it; my action is not modified' – the ability to do without it is not without its consolations either. Two stand out.

First, a high, dynamic doctrine of friendship will tend to value all kinds of friendship and refuse to allow any one to remain as 'mere' friendship. Rather, because such an attitude demands much of friendship, the result is that many good friendships are likely to be enjoyed. This is what is meant when we say someone has a gift for friendship: not that they necessarily have a soul friend but that they value friends.

Second, should it come about, soul friendship is not something that only benefits the individuals when actually possessed. Rather, when momentarily or over time two people form a connection unsullied by the usual ambiguous affections of life, free of the complexities of being honest, it is something that potentially stays with them for ever. We say that a connection has been made – 'we connected' – and the remembrance of that is in some ways as important as the moment itself. It is enough. As Menander once commented: 'A man is happy if he has merely encountered the shadow of a friend.'

Conclusion: Philosophy and Friendship

This book has been, I hope, a little bit of self-help, a little more technical philosophy, and mostly a search through the philosophical tradition and other cultural resources, to illuminate the perils and promise of friendship. I have had Tom Stoppard's comments in mind, when, reflecting on the philosophical romp that is his play *Jumpers* in a radio interview, he said:

> The area of moral philosophy [is] an open house for the layman, the non-philosopher, the curious human being because most of the questions which preoccupy professional philosophers are only an elevated more technical version of the kind of question which any sentient human being asks himself or herself while burning the toast.

When it comes to friendship, the questions are particularly close to most people's experience. Thus, first, I argued that friendship must engage with the utility-obsessed side of our culture, since, for all the good things it brings, the danger is that the law of productivity and consumption holds sway and friendship cannot rise above being instrumental; it risks being always determined by external workplace and workplace-like demands. If, though, individuals come to like one another for who they are, and not just for what they do, a better friendship becomes possible.

When it comes to friends and lovers, friendship's calling is to engage with the complex maelstrom of erotic feelings that can exist between two people and from that to discern a mutually shared passion that moves above the desire for romantic union to the desire to know (not to have) the other person, and be known by them. This higher passion is focused on things beyond the couple. It is, therefore, the same as that shared between friends who are lovers of life. It is sustainable, will grow, and should flourish.

Third, I argued that throughout pretty much all friendship runs the issue of dissimulation – the feigning that is kind, because even virtuous individuals find blunt honesty too harsh all of the time; that is wise, because even discerning individuals can make mistakes when judging others; and that is realistic, for most relationships depend upon a friendliness of measured not mounting affection. Once again, there is a promise that hides behind this peril: dissimulation can give way to honesty given the right circumstances, time and care. Candid friendships can transform a life with truthfulness.

The fourth ambiguity examined stemmed from the secular appropriation of Christianity's tendency to distrust friendship as a form of love. This can make moral philosophy suspicious of friendship in the way that marginalises and even outlaws it. What makes this particularly complicated is that it is the ethical systems that have given us universal rules and rights that are often the ones most antithetical to it. There are a number of ethical issues to contest if the value of friendship is to be revived: the subtle interplay of altruistic and egoistic motives are a major part of that. However, what is also vital is the factor identified by Thomas Aquinas, namely, the need to restore faith in the best sorts of friendship: this insight – found in the belief that God is friendship, or in secular guise as the conviction that ultimately friendship strives after that which is good – is key.

The politics of friendship is a similar kind of struggle to overcome. In one mode friendship resists the limiting constraints of inherited social conventions, notably in terms of the dictates of tight notions of family; in another mode it is a protest against individualistic, competitive conceptions of what it is to be human; and in another it is an effort to create new forms of relationship founded upon the freedom of friendships that go against the norm.

Finally, I have tried to outline a spirituality of friendship based upon the essays of Montaigne and Emerson. Success is found in circuit, to quote one poet. Or to use Keats's phrase, soul friendship would seem to be a prime candidate for his 'negative capability'.

Given that philosophy illuminates the nature, potential and limits of the love called friendship, there is one further, final observation to make. It centres on the figure of Socrates. He has regularly popped up throughout the course of the book. At one level, this is unsurprising; he is a major reference point in many philosophical discussions. But to see his presence here solely as a result of the fact that he is a big-hitter is to miss a more subtle point. For Socrates, I think, philosophy and friendship are ultimately one and the same thing.

According to Plato, Socrates understood the wily ambiguities of erotic love and argued that they should be seized upon as an opportunity to propel lovers along the wise course to a relationship based upon friendship. He also understood that true friendship is scarce. One may be friends with many, as indeed was he, the outcome of a way of life which took him around the streets of Athens seeking individuals to talk with. The complicating factor for him was that his vocation as a philosopher meant that he did not seek friends to be chummy but to encourage people to understand the errors in their beliefs and the failures of their character – in fact nothing less than the limits of their humanity. Rare is the individual who can embrace a relationship like that, and he was often left isolated, wondering whether he would ever find a true friend. At the same time, he never gave up hope.

Putting it another way, Socrates thought that friends should not primarily hope for happiness in one another, though that might come, but should seek together to live fuller, truer lives. This happens, he believed, when individuals become wise to their ignorance; the wisdom gained when one understands the limits of one's capabilities is more valuable than the facility for merely compounding proofs or facts. Such wisdom is best gained in discoursing with others, supremely so when the exchange is marked by the kind of honesty that can exist between the closest of friends. Then the individuals have the opportunity not only to learn about the limitations of the beliefs that they hold true but also about the flaws in their character and the vulnerabilities of their temperaments. These are, after all, far deeper sources of ignorance than mere rational confusion. Thus it is possible, I think, to construe the Socratic way of life as one that puts friendship centre stage. Epicurus, who in many ways followed in the same footsteps, agreed: 'The noble man is most involved with wisdom and friendship.'

This is a way of life based upon an ethos that moves from below up. The raw material of Socrates' philosophical work was not books, lectures or seminars but was the daily engagement of ordinary citizens, whether they had overtly philosophical aspirations or not. As Plutarch later put it:

Most people imagine that philosophy consists in delivering discourses from the heights of a chair, and in giving classes based on texts. But what these people utterly miss is the uninterrupted philosophy which we see being practised every day ... Socrates did not set up grandstands for his audience and did not sit upon a professorial chair; he had no fixed timetable for talking or walking with his friends. Rather he did philosophy sometimes by joking with them, or by drinking or going to war or to the market with them, and finally by going to prison and drinking poison. He was the first to show that at all times and in every place, in everything that happens to us, daily life gives us the opportunity to do philosophy.

Plato's dialogues deploy a number of metaphors and friendships that describe and portray Socrates' approach. Probably the most famous is that of the midwife: he takes his role to be that of one who knows he knows nothing but is committed to asking questions; sometimes his interlocutors 'give birth' to certain insights as a result – 'It is I, with God's help, who deliver them of this offspring [wisdom]', he says in the *Theaetetus*. Alternatively, in the *Meno*, Socrates describes his method by drawing a contrast with the eristic ways of his contemporary philosophical rivals, the sophists: 'If they are friends, as you and I are, and want to discuss with each other, they must answer in a manner more gentle and more proper to discussion.' The implication is that his way of doing philosophy is in part the attempt to form a friendship.

Socratic friendship is also a tough kind of love; it requires the roughest courage. Consider what he says to another character, Callicles, on the purpose of philosophy:

> I think that someone who is to test adequately the soul which lives aright and the soul which does not, needs to have three qualities: knowledge, goodwill and willingness to speak freely ... You [Callicles] would never have agreed with me simply because you did not know better or were too ashamed to admit you did not know, nor to deceive me; for you are my friend, as you say yourself.

As it happens Socrates is speaking ironically, for by the end of the dialogue in which this exchange is recorded, the *Gorgias*, Callicles has betrayed every one of the intimacies that they might have shared. His vanity could not take Socrates' probing enquiry. However, what Socrates says to Callicles reads like a summary of philosophy and friendship. It includes goodwill and a willingness to speak freely. It does not require individuals to be knowledgeable; rather they must have a passion for wisdom in Socrates' sense. Finally, the most promising candidates for friendship will show themselves to be honest, particularly when it comes to their self-awareness.

So it is not just Montaigne and Nietzsche, Emerson and Aelred who developed a dynamic ethos or spirituality of friendship characterised as the struggle to rise above life's everyday ambiguities. At the origins of Western philosophy is the same notion in which, at its best, doing philosophy and becoming friends are one and the same thing. Socratic friendship suggests that at least one conception of philosophy is itself caught up in this same dynamic. Friendship is the desire to know another and be known by them – in Emerson's phrase, they delight as they exclaim to one another, 'Do you see the same truth?' Philosophy is not, therefore, just illuminating of friendship. The very possibility of friendship lies at the heart of philosophy. They come together partly because as Aristotle commented, 'we are better able to observe our friends than ourselves and their actions than our own'. But more so because to truly befriend others is to stare life's uncertainties, limits and ambiguities in the face. To seek friendship is to seek wisdom.

Further Reading and References

Introduction: the ambiguity of friendship

Aristotle's examination of friendship is found in his *Nicomachean Ethics* chapters VIII and IX. A new translation, introduction and commentary by Sarah Broadie and Christopher Rowe published by Oxford University Press (2002) is clear and helpful. All my quotes from Aristotle come from this *Ethics* unless stated. He does discuss friendship elsewhere, notably in the *Eudemian Ethics* which is usually taken to be the main source for the *Nicomachean Ethics*. And also in the *Art of Rhetoric* 6.2.4.

The thought experiment of Nietzsche is from *Human, All Too Human* Volume I, 376.

1. Friends at work

The Aristotle references are from his *Nicomachean Ethics* chapters VIII and IX.

The Theory of Moral Sentiments, by Adam Smith, is available from a number of publishers and can also be downloaded; Prometheus Books produce a cheap edition. An academic but readable article, 'Adam Smith on Friendship and Love', by Douglas J. Den Uyl and Charles L. Griswold Jr., can be found in the *Review of Metaphysic* 49 (March 1996): 609–37.

Smith is compared with Ferguson and Hume in Lisa Hill and Peter McCarthy's article 'Hume, Smith and Ferguson: Friendship in Commercial Society', in the excellent book *The Challenge to Friendship in Modernity*, edited by Preston King and Heather Devere and published by Frank Cass (2000).

Friendship at work as an area of research has established quite a niche for itself in many business schools. Geraldine Perreault of the University of Northern Iowa, for example, has written on leadership as friendship.

2. Friends and lovers

Montaigne's essay 'On Friendship' where he discusses his relationship with La Boëtie can be found in any collection of his *Complete Essays*, though Penguin's Great Ideas series includes an attractive publication of it alone, if without introduction.

John Evelyn and Margaret Godolphin's friendship is examined in wonderful detail by Frances Harris in *Transformations of Love*, published by Oxford University Press (2002).

Simon Callow's *Love Is Where It Falls: an Account of a Passionate Friendship* is a highly readable, witty and moving book published by Penguin (1999).

C. S. Lewis's essay on friendship in *The Four Loves* (reissued in HarperCollins Signature Classics edition, 2002) is idiosyncratic and insightful in equal measure.

The quotes from Nietzsche are from *The Gay Science* Book 1, 14. The classic on Greek homosexuality is Kenneth Dover's eponymous book (Duckworth, 1997), though James Davidson's forthcoming *The Greeks and Greek Love* (Weidenfeld and Nicolson, 2006) is set to revise that view.

There are many discussions of Plato's ideas about love; any introduction to Plato will include one. The translations of the *Symposium* and the *Phaedrus*, by Alexander Nehamas and Paul Woodruff, are engaging with accessible introductions. Martha Nussbaum is an oft-quoted source too: *The Fragility of Goodness* (Cambridge University Press, 1986) contains many illuminating discussions.

When it comes to Plato on friendship in particular (and his dialogue the *Lysis*) there are fewer choices. The first chapter of Lorraine Smith Pangle's *Aristotle and the Philosophy of Friendship* (Cambridge University Press, 2003) is an academic examination of the *Lysis*, as is Anthony Price's rich and challenging first chapter in *Love and Friendship in Plato and Aristotle* (Clarendon Press, 1990). My appendix here offers a more accessible outline, though one that may be contested by some. For another alternative translation and commentary on the dialogue David Bolotin captures the drama as well as the philosophy – *Plato's Dialogue on Friendship* (Cornell University Press, 1979).

For general philosophical comparisons of love and friendship I enjoyed Allan Bloom's *Love and Friendship* (Simon & Schuster, 1993) and the chapter on love in Andre Comte-Sponville's *A Short Treatise on the Great Virtues* (Vintage, 2003), though I am not sure he gets friendship quite right. Alain de Botton's *Essays in Love* (Picador, 1994) is an excellent novelised portrayal of love that touches on friendship too.

3. Faking it

The quotes from Nietzsche in this chapter come from three books, unless otherwise stated. A more or less complete list of his aphorisms on friendship in this middle period is:

Human, All Too Human Volume I, 354, 368, 376, 378, 390, 406, 499; Volume II, 241, 242, 251, 259, 260.

The Gay Science Book 1, 14, 16; Book 2, 61; Book 4, 279, 328; Book 5, 364, 366; and from the Prelude, Rhymes 14 and 25.

Daybreak Book 4, 287, 313; Book 5, 489.

Ruth Abbey puts them into academic context in her article 'Circles, Ladders and Stars: Nietzsche on Friendship', in *The Challenge to Friendship in Modernity*, edited by Preston King and Heather Devere, published by Frank Cass (2000).

Proust's attitude to friendship is examined in Duncan Large's 'Proust on Nietzsche: the Question of Friendship', *Modern Language Review*, 88/3 (July 1993): 612–24.

For more on Stanley Cavell's thoughts his *Conditions Handsome and Unhandsome: the Constitution of Emersonian Perfectionism* (University of Chicago Press, 1991) is a good place to start.

4. Unconditional love

Maria Boulding's translation of Augustine's *Confessions* (Hodder and Stoughton, 1997) captures the remarkably modern feel of the autobiography. Peter Brown's classic biography of the saint is called *Augustine of Hippo: a Biography* (Faber and Faber, 1967).

The relevant sections from Kierkegaard's *Works of Love* are usefully collated in *Other Selves: Philosophers on Friendship*, edited by Michael Pakaluk and published by Hackett (1991).

As indeed are the key paragraphs from Thomas's *Summa Theologiae*. For an examination of his philosophy and theology, Brian Davies's *The Thought of Thomas Aquinas* (Clarendon, 1993) is hard to beat.

The Kant lecture is in Pakaluk's book too with an introduction.

Alasdair MacIntyre's reflections come from *After Virtue* (University of Notre Dame Press, 1984).

To follow up on Iris Murdoch's idea of the good, see *The Sovereignty of Good* (Routledge, 1970).

Few contemporary Christian writers have sought to reconcile friendship and theology at book length which is itself notable given the ink spilt on divine love. P. Waddell's *Friendship and the Moral Life* (University of Notre Dame Press, 1989) and G. Meilaender's *Friendship: a Study in Theological Ethics* (University of Notre Dame Press, 1981) are two that are often cited. For a latter-day Kierkegaard, see Anders Nygren's *Agape and Eros*. *Friendship and the Ways to Truth*, by David Burrell (University of Notre Dame Press, 2000), weaves philosophy and faith together. Elizabeth Stuart's *Just Good Friends* (Mowbray, 1995) approaches the issue from a lesbian and gay perspective. Stanley Hauerwas has an article 'Companions on the Way: the Necessity of Friendship', in *The Ashbury Theological Journal* Vol. 45 (1990): 1. My Postscript to Jeremy Carrette's book *Religion and Culture by Michel Foucault* (Routledge, 1999), 'I Am Not What Am', offers a view of friendship through theological eyes.

5. Civic friendship

David Konstan's *Friendship in the Classical World* (Cambridge University Press, 1997) discusses everything you could want to know about the matter and more. G. Herman in *Ritualised Friendship and the Greek City* (Cambridge University Press, 1987) is anthropological. Paul Cartledge's *The Greeks: a Portrait of Self and Others* (Oxford University Press, 1993) paints the broader picture.

The Aristotle references are from his *Nicomachean Ethics* Chapter VIII and his civic friendship is discussed by Richard Mulgan in his article 'The Role of Friendship in Aristotle's Political Theory', in *The Challenge to Friendship in Modernity*, edited by Preston King and Heather Devere. David Cohen in *Law, Sexuality and Society: the Enforcement of Morals in Classical Athens* (Cambridge University Press, 1991) is fascinating on the place of the household in political friendships.

The longest discussion of friendship in Plato's *Republic* occurs in Book 1 [334b ff], though not directly in relation to the ideal city-state. In the *Laws*, friendship is raised in a variety of contexts, for example, at [693c], [729d], [738d–e], [743c] and [757a].

The surviving texts of Epicurus are available in a number of readers. Suzanne Stern-Gillet brings Epicurean friendship to life, given the limited sources, in an article 'Epicurus and Friendship', in the journal *Dialogue*, 28 (1989): 275–88.

Cicero's dialogue on friendship, *Laelius*, can be found in the Penguin Classics volume *On the Good Life* (translated by Michael Grant, 1971).

Alan Bray's *The Friend* is published by University of Chicago Press (2003). Diarmuid MacCulloch's *Reformation: Europe's House Divided* (Penguin, 2004) discusses changing attitudes to love, family and marriage. John Bossy's *Christianity in the West 1400–1700* (Oxford University Press, 1985) captures the essence and function of the medieval notion of charity. John Boswell's *Same-Sex Unions in Premodern Europe* (Vintage, 1995) offers an alternative, and to my mind slightly less convincing, account of sworn friendship.

Frances Bacon's essay 'Of Friendship' addresses the particular issue of friendship with kings. (It can be found in any collection of his essays. Everyman publish a cheap edition.) His point is that those who are otherwise above reproach because of the power they wield need friends in order to keep their feet on the ground. Friendship, as Bacon puts it, 'opens the understanding', 'waxeth wiser', and 'there is no such remedy against flattery of a man's self as the liberty of a friend'. However, this friend cum special advisor on personal integrity can only speak the truth to power because he has minimal political interests of his own. If political concerns influence the friend, his advice loses its personal edge and his intimacy becomes sycophancy; friendship matters to Bacon because it is above affairs of state.

John Locke's *Essay concerning the True Original, Extent, and End of Civil Government* is available online for free.

There is an interesting discussion of Anselm on friendship in an article entitled 'Friendship', by David Moss, in *Radical Orthodoxy*, edited by John Milbank, Catherine Pickstock and Graham Ward (Routledge, 1998).

Aelred's *Spiritual Friendship* is available from Cistercian Publications. Exerpts can be found in *Other Selves: Philosophers on Friendship*, edited by Michael Pakaluk.

I Know My Own Heart: the Diaries of Anne Lister, 1791–1840 is published by Virago (1988). Bray discusses the relationship at length.

6. Politics of friendship

Michael Farrell's *Collaborative Circles: Friendship Dynamics and Creative Work* is published by University of Chicago Press (2003). My quotes come from his book. *Not For Ourselves Alone*, a film of Stanton and Anthony's life from PBS, is available on DVD from Warner Home Video.

Lillian Faderman's *Surpassing the Love of Men: Romantic Friendship and Love between Women from the Renaissance to the Present* is published by HarperCollins (1998). The quote of Simone de Beauvoir comes from *The Second Sex* (Vintage Classics, 1997).

Marilyn Friedman's essay 'Feminism and Modern Friendship: Dislocating the Community' can be found in a mixed collection of essays, *Friendship: a Philosophical Reader*, edited by Neera Kapur Badhwar (Cornell University Press, 1993).

Mary E. Hunt discusses her politics of friendship in *Fierce Tenderness: a Feminist Theology of Friendship* (Crossroad, 1991).

My discussion of molly houses draws historical material from David Greenberg's *The Construction of Homosexuality* (University of Chicago Press, 1988). Michael Vasey's interpretation of their significance is in *Strangers and Friends* (Hodder and Stoughton, 1995).

For more on Mark Simpson see www.marksimpson.com.

Love Undetectable: Reflections on Friendship, Sex and Survival, by Andrew Sullivan, is where his discussion of gay friendship can be found (Vintage, 1999).

Foucault's work on friendship can be hard to find, especially since it has become fashionable to attribute extreme constructionist accounts of sexuality to him. However, the thoughtful interview 'Friendship as a Way of Life' is in *Foucault Live*, edited by S. Lotringer (Semiotext(e), 1989). Jeremy Carrette's *Religion and Culture by Michel Foucault* (Routledge, 1999) also contains useful material.

Jeffrey Weeks's research is published in *Same-Sex Intimacies: Families of Choice and Other Life Experiments* (Routledge, 2001). Anthony Giddens's ideas are found in *The Transformation of Intimacy* (Stanford University Press, 1993).

Liz Spencer and Ray Pahl's latest research is due out as *Hidden Solidarities: Friendship and Personal Communities Today* in 2005 from Princeton University Press. Pahl's *On Friendship* (Polity Press, 2000) is an accessible essay on friendship with a sociological slant.

For a less empirical take, try *Bowling Along*, by Robert Putnam (Simon and Schuster, 2000).

7. The spirituality of friendship

The quote of Richard Wollheim comes from Chapter IX of *The Thread of Life* (Yale University Press, 1999).

Montaigne's essay 'On Friendship' can be found in any collection of his *Complete Essays*, and Penguin's Great Ideas series includes an edition of it alone.

Emerson's essay 'Friendship' comes from his First Series and is in *The Essential Writings of Ralph Waldo Emerson* (Modern Library, 2000), edited by Brooks Atkinson and with an introduction by Mary Oliver, whom I quote too. *The Woman and the Myth: Margaret Fuller's Life and Writings*, edited by Bell Gale Chevigny (Northeastern University Press, 1994), provides much more about Fuller.

Conclusion: philosophy and friendship

Plutarch says this of Socrates in 'Whether a Man should Engage in Politics When He is Old', 26, 796d.

For more on the Socratic way of life though not so much on friendship, Pierre Hadot's *What Is Ancient Philosophy?* (Belknap Press, 2004) is a great read.

Appendix: Plato and Aristotle on Friendship

For most philosophies of friendship, Aristotle provides the touchstone. His account of friendship, it is commonplace to argue, is the most penetrating analysis of friendship in ancient philosophy.

He begins with a definition of friendship; here is the succinct version found in the *Eudemian Ethics* (of which the *Nicomachean Ethics* is usually taken to be a reworking) – 'A man becomes a friend whenever being loved he loves in return' [*EE* 1236a14]. He divides friendship into three types. The first are utility-based friendships, like those of the workplace, where the friendship rests on a mutual benefit. The second are pleasure-based friendships, like those between young lovers, where the friendship rests on a shared pleasure. The third are friendships of excellence, meaning that the relationship stems from the excellent qualities that the friends embody in themselves. In terms of my discussion, these are like the friends who know each other well, can be honest and truthful to one another, and therefore exhibit other virtues such as those listed by Aristotle, including courage, great-spiritedness and generosity. Thus Aristotle sums up in the *Eudemian Ethics*: 'If there is to be friendship, the parties must have goodwill towards each other, i.e. wish good things for each other, and be aware of the other's doing so, the feeling being brought about by one of the three things mentioned [the beneficial, pleasant or good]' [*EE* 1156a4].

This provides a framework from within which Aristotle can examine many aspects of friendship, material that I have drawn on extensively. It allows him to write evocative, even sublime aphorisms on what, after all, should be a beautiful subject: 'No one would choose to live without friends, even if he had all the other goods' [*NE* 1155a2]; 'For though the wish for friendship arises quickly, friendship does not' [*NE* 1156b32]; 'A friend is another self' [*NE* 1170b7].

However, this approach has its limits, of which Aristotle was undoubtedly aware. We noted one at the outset; that for the very best of friendships, the suggestion that they are based on goodwill seems rather to miss the point (like saying a painting is just oil on canvas, or a book just words on the page).

But, there are more profound philosophical problems with his account. In Book X of the *Nicomachean Ethics*, the final book, Aristotle comes to what he thinks is the best life of all. It is the contemplative life, a life spent in as full a state of consciousness as possible of those things that are thought truest. There are a number of reasons why Aristotle comes to this conclusion. First, those things that are truest must be the most excellent of all, and so make for the greatest happiness. Second, those things that are truest must be the most dependable things of all and so be reliable, again making for happiness. And third, contemplating those things can be done without having to depend on others: this means that such a person's happiness does not depend on others and so is free of the unhappiness that others are bound to precipitate from time to time.

But this begs a question that is problematic for friendship: if someone does not need others to be happy then why would they need friends at all, or at least would not the friendship they offered others be somewhat half-hearted?

Aristotle is aware of the problem and in the course of the chapters on friendship he offers several suggestions. For example, it may be that for most human beings the contemplative state can only be achieved some of the time. Much of the time, therefore, people will need friends to be happy. Alternatively, it could be that human beings need others to learn how to perceive those things that are the truest, especially when it comes to freeing themselves from self-delusion. To that extent they will need friends.

Another possible way out for him arises from an ambiguity in the *Nicomachean Ethics* as a whole. For whilst he suggests in Book X that the contemplative life is the happiest, in the earlier part of the *Ethics* he suggests that a life lived actively with others can be as happy since it makes for its own kinds of practical excellences [*NE* 1095b18 ff]. This is undoubtedly true. Take friendship. I have argued that it is itself a school of love and virtue. However, Aristotle is very keen on those contemplative insights in Book X; they are divine, he says. So, again, a certain ambiguity remains as to quite how important friendship can actually be for the happiest of lives.

In other words, the supposed solution to his problem actually makes the situation worse. His approach rests upon a definition of friendship, and from that points to the quintessential kind – shared between those living the best life possible. However, if this quintessential case is itself compromised, because the greatest happiness is achieved by self-sufficient individuals, then it seems that his whole theory of friendship is under threat.

Aristotle's is not the only considered account of friendship in antiquity. Plato provides another, in the shape of his dialogue, the *Lysis*. The *Lysis* is often overlooked by philosophers for a number of reasons. First, it is not so much an account of friendship as a portrayal of friendship, and as such may be less appealing to the contemporary analytical frame of mind. Second, in the same way that it is a portrayal not an account, it is also a philosophical drama and not a philosophical treatise. In other words, the actions of the characters and the cultural and social inferences within the dialogue may count as much for its meaning as anything the participants actually say. This, again, means that it can be taken to be less definitive. Indeed, as we have seen, it ends aporetically – that is, Socrates says to his interlocutors that although they intuitively think they know what friendship is, what it actually is they have not been able to say. Philosophers, including Aristotle, have therefore tended to conclude that the *Lysis* contains a few useful comments in terms of identifying certain problems associated with love and friendship, but that ultimately it is flawed. For Plato's best account of love one must turn to his philosophical masterpiece, the *Symposium*.

But I think that if the *Lysis* can be accused of anything it is only of hiding its light under a bushel. And what is more, given a certain reading of it, it can be seen to be at its most successful precisely at the points where Aristotle stumbles. Here's what happens.

The dialogue opens with Socrates one day walking through Athens. He comes across two young men, Hippothales and Ctesippus, who are hanging around outside a gymnasium, partly to talk and partly to observe the youths coming and going. Socrates teases them about which activity they prefer and it turns out that one of them, Hippothales, is infatuated with one of the students inside, the beautiful Lysis. This is actually completely obvious, although when Socrates spots it, it does give him the opportunity ironically to add that although he is ignorant about all things – his wisdom stemming from knowing that he knows nothing – there is one area in which he does have some insight, and that is in matters of love. So, Hippothales asks Socrates how to woo Lysis.

Socrates begins by exploring the nature of Hippothales' infatuation. Ctesippus says that its most painful feature is that it causes Hippothales to sing insufferable songs, comparing Lysis to a summer's day (not that, of course: the ancient Mediterranean motif appears to have been comparison with a fine horseman). Socrates is saved having to listen to these odes, but he agrees they are embarrassing (for the same reason that infatuation is demeaning). First, they show that Hippothales knows nothing special about Lysis: everyone knows the line about the fine horsemen. Secondly, they show he knows nothing about himself: he is singing as if he has already won Lysis' love, something that will not only be painful if he fails to do so, and also something that is a strategic mistake since, like a hunter who sings in the forest, he is likely to scare his prey away before he gets near him. In short, infatuation is not true love, it is blind love. There are wise words here for those prone to the infatuated state. Having made his point, Socrates then agrees to show Hippothales how it should be done. They go into the gymnasium and find Lysis.

This marks the end of the introductory section of the dialogue [203a–206e], for we now meet the youth himself. When he appears, he does not disappoint. But Socrates then does a surprising thing. Rather than wooing Lysis, he starts to talk to Lysis' friend Menexenus, who has also joined them. Moreover, Socrates asks Menexenus about his friendship with Lysis, something that continues when Menexenus turns to Lysis and brings him into the conversation. In other words, Socrates is saying to Hippothales, if you want to love him, don't fawn all over him, but befriend him. The dialogue has switched to its main subject, friendship.

Before continuing with what happens next, it is worth asking why Plato devised an apparently roundabout route to approach his subject. The answer is that Socrates does not know what friendship is in itself. For all that he might have an idea, perhaps drawing on the experience of having friends, his wisdom tells him that it is likely to be wrong. If, therefore, he had begun by proposing a definition, for example, there would be no guarantee that it was not a misleading false start.

However, he needs to begin somehow: there clearly are things to be said about friendship. So, he begins with the one thing he does know about, namely, love. Socrates knows about love because he takes love, at base, to be the desire for something that someone lacks. For example, someone who is in love wants their beloved and, even when they are together, they want them forever (that is, not lacking them at some point in the future). Similarly, Socrates knows about love because he is a philosopher of the sort who longs for the truth, perceiving that he lacks it. Thus, knowing about love is paradoxically consistent with knowing too that one is ignorant.

What the initial encounter with Hippothales shows is that being infatuated is doubly ignorant: the person who is infatuated neither really knows the person they love nor perceives that they do not. Socrates can show that much to Hippothales with confidence; he wants to inculcate in him a wiser love.

Now, Socrates suspects that this wiser love might be something to do with friendship. He has, after all, spent his life wandering around Athens, and the people with whom he has had the most philosophically illuminating conversations have often become friends. But he does not know what friendship is in itself. So, Plato contrives for Socrates now to meet not only Lysis but also Lysis' friend, Menexenus. They are youths and full of youthful friendship, we might say of the sort that are made between first-year undergraduates, based upon the foolish assumption that all things are possible, all things are pleasurable and nothing can possibly separate the friends. In other words, it is an obvious candidate for friendship but one that has the virtue, as far as the Socratic way of doing philosophy is concerned, of being equally obviously flawed (like the best scientific theories, its value lies in being readily falsified). It therefore provides a good place to start an examination of friendship. We might note that this is very much like the 'from-below-up' idea of friendship that lies at the heart of the Emersonian spirituality of friendship.

Sure enough, Socrates looks at the friends in front of him – Lysis and Menexenus – and asks them about their particular friendship [207b ff]. He teases them about it, playing on its competitive character; he asks them who is the more beautiful, wealthy and wise. They try to laugh this off (shallow friendship has few resources for facing such questions) and immediately start to feel uneasy about their relationship. The brilliance of this move philosophically speaking is that Plato has therefore already taken a step forward – Socrates is more interested in a deeper kind of friendship than the one displayed in front of him – but without making any presuppositions.

The opportunity to take another step comes next because Menexenus is called off to do something else in the gymnasium, leaving Lysis free to talk to Socrates on his own [207d–210e]. The 'from-below-up' approach comes into its own now: Socrates does not ask Lysis about friendship per se but starts to converse with him with the aim of befriending him. (Moreover, a philosophical discussion about friendship would be a dry thing if it was not at least open to the possibility of friendship forming between the interlocutors.) Though, Socrates' technique for befriending Lysis seems at first to be more likely to provoke antagonism not amity. For example, he forces Lysis to admit that although he comes from a rich and privileged family, he is barely free to do or think anything of his own volition because his parents and guardians watch over him in nearly every respect. This is strong stuff for a young Athenian male whose education was nothing if not a preparation for the life of politics and pleasure. However, Lysis is a humble chap. He can take Socrates disabusing him of his self-delusion. And, in fact, implicitly thanks Socrates for doing so. Needless to say, Socrates warms to this response very much, and so although he set out challenging Lysis, the beginnings of a deeper friendship are the result. Had he merely chatted to him, their relationship would have remained friendly but ephemeral.

Menexenus then returns [211a]. This is the point at which Socrates makes his dramatic confession [211d]. He declares that he knows nothing about friendship, though he would rather have a friend than all the gold of the king of Persia, Darius: 'I don't even know the manner in which one becomes a friend of another', he says. 'When it comes to the acquisition of friends [I am] quite passionately in love' – that is, he lacks friendship and longs for it. As we noted before, this is a very strong admission. It places his desire for a friend and for an understanding of friendship on a par with the passionate love that has defined his life, his desire for wisdom; not so surprising given that the relationship between Socratic philosophy and friendship is in many ways one of correspondence.

This confession is of course somewhat ironic, and for the same reason that Emerson advocated a paradoxical stance. Socrates does have friends but he does not enjoy a friendship of the highest sort.

It also serves to draw a contrast with the friendship between Menexenus and Lysis, the friendship of a rather boyish, immature sort: what Socrates wants is not mere friendship but friendship of the sort that can embrace human uncertainty and life's imperfections. Perhaps Lysis has already started to realise this given his conversation with Socrates and sees now that Socrates is calling his friendship with Menexenus into question by suggesting that something better should be possible.

What, then, might this be like? What is true friendship and who is a good friend? A good friend must be wise, in the way that Socrates is wise, and the conversation between Socrates, Lysis and Menexenus now explores what this means for friendship in some depth. Socrates says that he occupies what he calls an 'in-between' state [216c ff]. On the one hand, his wisdom is not god-like: he knows one thing, that he is ignorant. If he knew more, he would not be a philosopher – one who searches for wisdom. Moreover, he would have no reason to seek out deeper friendships because his philosophical quest would cease (like Aristotle's self-sufficient individual, the rest of his life would be one of contemplation). On the other hand, if he knew nothing and was blind to the fact, he would not be a philosopher either; he would be just an opinionated old man. In this case, his desire for friendship of any significant sort would be dramatically reduced too because he would not entertain, let alone seek out, individuals who challenged his ignorance. Socrates is in-between these states, being mostly uncertain about things and aware of his limits. It is this state of being, this negative capability, which makes for the best possibilities of friendship.

Socrates demonstrates what he means in another way, by asking Lysis and Menexenus who they think might make good friends [212b–216c]. They discuss various options. For example, do people who are alike befriend one another well, as in the saying 'like with like together strike'. This seems a strong possibility though they then realise that people who are wholly alike have little to offer one another because the other person will have it already. Since friends are a good thing to have in part because they can be useful to each other (whilst not being *merely* useful to each other), then it is hard to see how individuals who are too alike can make for the deepest kind of friendship. Indeed, it is often said that animosity springs up between people when they are too alike.

So maybe, they wonder, the best kinds of friendship form between individuals who are unalike – as the dry desert welcomes rain, or the cold day sunshine. This seems possible, as in the saying 'opposites attract'. But the individuals must not be so unlike each other that they have nothing in common. And if in the logical extreme one was led to presume that friendship would form between those who are wholly unalike, then this would clearly be as ridiculous as saying that enemies were friends.

If these intellectual rambles might seem like the kind of thing that philosopher friends would enjoy together, but not others, then there is a deeper reason for running through them. Remember, Socrates is now talking with two individuals who have begun to question the veracity of their friendship. One relatively kind way of encouraging them to think about that is to explore the sorts of conditions that make for friendship in abstract. In asking whether friends are alike, Lysis and Menexenus are bound to wonder whether that is the basis, and perhaps the problem, with their friendship. Similarly, in asking about the relationship between people who are unalike. This approach also has benefits for the reader of the dialogue because they too are encouraged to compare the friendships they enjoy with what is being said. Plato hopes, I think, that his readers may learn something not only about friendship per se, but also more importantly about the dynamics of their own friendships.

In other words, it carries the advantages of a below-up ethos of friendship. By toying with possibilities for friendship – between like, unalike and so on – one is learning to be open to the ways in which various scenarios in real life might contain the seeds of deeper friendship. The general point is that life causes many people to cross our path. When it comes to seeking friendship, the best way is not to try to impose some predetermined idea of friendship on the people we meet: like saying happiness is such and such, that way only brings disappointment. Rather, it is to assess the various encounters that life brings, with all their ambiguities, uncertainties and possibilities, and ask, who are my good friends and why – what can I nurture about them? This is, again, good advice in a sentimental age with a tendency to avoid the real in preference for idealised relationships and individuals. It is exactly the opposite approach to the self-help book that advises drawing up lists of 3 'must-haves', 3 'nice-to-haves', and 3 'avoid at all costs' and then advises seeking this 'perfect' person out.

There is more to this Socratic friendship for other reasons too. For example, it emphasises the fact that there is always more to discover, and enjoy, in the friendship. This is another positive aspect to the scarcity of the very best kind. What Plato implies in the *Lysis* is that friendship is a way of life, in the sense of being a constant process of becoming with others. Sparked by desire, like other loves, it is distinguished by a dynamic that results in an increasing self-awareness coupled to knowing the other better. Friends want to know each other and be known. Like the lovers who become friends too, because they turn from gazing into each other's eyes to appreciate the world around them, the best friendships are not confined to a mutual introspection; they are fed by a common striving after those goals, hopes and excellent things which lie beyond and around them. (In the *Lysis*, this aspect comes through when they discuss what drives friendship, calling it the 'first love' or *proton philon* [219c].)

Further, it is to acknowledge the mystery of loving another deeply – a mystery because ultimately there are always parts of them that are unknown. This may be a hard thing to accept if friendship is sought solely for security. But the great thing about acknowledging it is that the limit it apparently imposes paradoxically turns out to make for the very best friendships. Think of it another way: although best friends say they know each other, they do not say there is nothing more to discover about you or learn from you. Apart from the insult, that would suggest that they are bored of the friendship; once admitted, the friendship would unravel. Rather, the motor of friendship is the delight of always finding more in the friend and in friendship. Friendship is, then, a way of life that is always deepening and broadening itself.

It is for this reason that the *Lysis* ends with the aporia [223a ff]. Trivially, it makes the point that the friendship between Socrates and Lysis can only get so far in one encounter, and perhaps even additional meetings are likely to be limited because Lysis is young (Plato has Socrates speculating 'off-camera' that he might have to seek older individuals out to pursue friendship further). But more substantially, it shows that any good friendship will be open ended, as the dialogue is.

So, the *Lysis* offers a portrayal of friendship as a way of life in which, at its best, Socratic philosophy and becoming friends are one and the same thing. What is more, it does not face the problems Aristotle does. In Socrates' scheme of things, there is no such thing as the self-sufficient person who can happily contemplate truth free of doubt. Further, any attempt to conclusively define friendship fails too: else it would share the same risk that actual friends do if they congratulate themselves on the fullness, depth and perfection of their friendship: they would have settled for less than the fullness of life which is an ongoing process of becoming – 'I could do the best good for each of you, by persuading you to be less concerned with what you have than with what you are, so that you may make yourself excellent in wisdom and truth and the perfection of your soul' [*Apology* 29e].

Index